THE CHIEF OF BIRDS

Copyright 2023 © Michael Templeton

ISBN: 978-1-916541-00-9

First edition.

All rights reserved.

First published in 2023 by Erratum Press
Sheffield, UK
www.erratumpress.com

Design and typesetting by Ansgar Allen
Cover image Michael Templeton

THE CHIEF OF BIRDS
A MEMOIR

Michael Templeton

ERRATUM PRESS

Preface

The House (as I will call it from here on) has saved countless men over the years of its existence. I want to emphasize that. I would not be here today were it not for the House, and I know a great many men who would be dead, on the street, or in prison were it not for the House. I want to make this clear.

I cannot account for how or why my experiences became what they were; why I saw things the ways that I did while others were able to sail through it all without a second thought. It would take another book to unpack the features and experiences from my life that disposed me to experience life in rehab the way I did. However, I am not going to apologize for how I experienced these things. Whatever "humility" may be demanded to accept things without question or resistance is foreign to me, and I do not make this statement with pride or remorse. It simply is a fact.

I wrote this the only way I could. Everything that happened, all the experiences, thoughts, feelings, ideas—all of it is lost in a mix of post-addiction pathology and a life that was foreign to me at every moment I lived it. If the book refuses a narrative structure, that is because I had no narrative or structure to assemble. All that happened was either a jumble of fragments or moments that resemble the dead air of a radio station that is not tuned to anything. Blank spaces and fractured experiences are all I had. Even with the help of the numerous journals I filled while I lived at the House, nothing can be retrieved in a coherent fashion. The only thing that offered, and still offers, some kind of logic or sense are the books I relied on during my time there. Most important of those books are the works of Samuel Beckett. And I cannot explain why those made sense over everything else.

If you read the works of Beckett, and if you continue on and read some of the critical studies of his work, one thing that comes up repeatedly is that you cannot really say anything about the works of Samuel Beckett. Even those critics who advanced complex theses on what one can say about Samuel Beckett invariably pull punches and admit that any conclusions they arrived at are provisional at best. I found something in Beckett that provided a voice for myself where I had come to experience my own voice as effectively silenced. I took the imaginary voice of silence as the voice of my silence.

It is not as though I found a grand figure of identification in Beckett, although I did occasionally identify with characters and sentiments expressed by them. I had never read Beckett before coming to the House, and I certainly never studied his work. I also knew almost nothing about his life. The first book I read was *How it is*. I don't even remember where I found it. This book never expresses a complete thought, and the fragments of thoughts it does express are repeated with variations until whatever meaning they contained is washed out. I think it is this process of laundering speech until it is blank that spoke to me, and still does.

The book is peppered with quotations from the works of Samuel Beckett. Since my "I" had been so thoroughly effaced by external systems of meaning, by language that became more official and real than my own, I ceased to see a difference between my own words and the words of others. As an act of defiance, I let the words of Samuel Beckett speak for me. It is analogous to the way Roland Barthes interpolates other forms of textuality into his own in the course of *A Lover's Discourse*. It is also my way of simply saying nuts to anyone or anything that would demand that I make sense in a conventional way.

Long after I left the House, I discovered the works of Maurice Blanchot. *The Writing of the Disaster* became something of a road map for how I would finally write this book. I will make no attempt to explain Beckett or Blanchot. I make no claim to even properly understand either. What I will insist is that those who lay claim to ways of reading and understanding that operate in the manner of mastery are simply false. What an author meant is what the author said. Everything else is speculation at best, and I say this as one who has the credentials to speak with mastery about literature and philosophy. I did not read Beckett and later Blanchot. I experienced them. And that is all I can say. Read them yourself. Experience them yourself.

The Chief of Birds

> To write one's autobiography, in order either to confess or to engage in self-analysis, or in order to expose oneself, like a work of art, to the gaze of all, is perhaps to seek to survive, but through a perpetual suicide—a death which is total inasmuch as fragmentary.
>
> Blanchot, *The Writing of the Disaster*

The writing of myself began well before I set out to write a memoir. Put another way, I found that I had been written before I began to write. The self that remained, having been effaced along several trajectories, was spontaneously and almost randomly re-assembled from fragments that belonged to others. And assembling a self from fragments, I cannot tell the tale except as fragments. I do not have a unified story to tell, and what remained of the life that preceded all of this was splintered into countless pieces none of which are my own. When I reached the end, I had little of myself to work with. I had become unrecognizable to myself. I found that I had entered the flow of processes that took no account of my sense of myself; they took no account of mine or anyone else's. I found that I already existed elsewhere in the documents and designations of systems that precede and exceed me. I might well have created a self at one time, but this had all become superfluous. In place of a lack, I did not seek to re-create, or even create, a self, but rather the words by which I might create something in place of a self. Without realizing what I was doing, I began assembling fragments of things written by others in order to form something entirely unconnected to the shards of myself that I still remembered.

I was effaced, or displaced, first by a disease, if we are to accept the language of the medical establishment, then by the systems designed to return me to life as a more settled and adjusted adult. Addiction is most often referred to as a disease, but the medical and psychiatric communities now differ as to the exact nature of what I lived with. In any case, where I ended up categorized me completely under the rubric of disease. Anything I felt, thought, believed, all of my actions, all of my personal attachments, my loves and hates—everything became features of my disease. My "self" was negated as the language of recovery took over everything I believed made me exist. A self, a living body in the world, the presence of a living body, is negated by a kind of suicide, or murder as the case may be, in order for that living body to take up the intimate features of a self into the realm of language which refuses the living presence of a self. I had, like everyone, an internal and constantly shifting sense of myself, that indeterminate quilt of memories, memories of memories, experiences, beliefs, fears, hopes, dreams, distant and pre-memorial imprints and infantile sensations, etc. All of this existed in language and language systems that I actively engaged, created, re-created, resisted, shaped, etc. The structural integrity of this tissue of knowledge was shattered and even nullified upon reaching the end in the form of my entry into the House. Everything was superseded by other language systems and tissues of knowledge (complete with the power embedded in knowledge) over and above whatever I once assumed to be myself. My living presence was marked as the absent center within the contents of language systems that nullified my presence. This is death as life that is taken over and over-written from the outside. The only thing left for me was to subtract something that could stand in for a self, to steal pieces of language in order to create something from less than nothing. There is the self, and there is the representation of the self in language which is not alive and has no presence. "Every life is many days, day after day. We walk through ourselves, meeting robbers, ghosts, giants, old men, young men, wives, widows, brothers-in-love. But always meeting ourselves" (Joyce, *Ulysses*, 191). The language which tells the tale of the self is the mark of the absence of the presence of the self. I am working with what remained of a self after other dimensions had been abstracted and negated by a medical system which rendered me an object of the gaze. What I was compelled to do was subtract a self from these external language systems and supplement what had been subtracted with language I found in still other domains, which could provide a language system by which I could come to recognize and define a self from within… "the lord of all things as they are whom the most Roman of catholics call *dio boia*, hangman god, is doubtless all in all of us, ostler and butcher, would be bawd and cuckold too but in the economy of heaven, foretold by Hamlet, there are no more marriages, glorified men, an androgynous angel, being a wife unto himself" (*Ulysses,* 192).

Giving myself over to a mode of understanding that defines me within a system of disease necessarily means allowing all forms of self-definition to be blotted out. My desires and drives are now the pathological compulsions of a disease. All internal feelings are transformed into symptoms.

Anger, frustration, resentment, but also love, lust, passion, sympathy, and compassion—whether directed outward or inward, everything is now the manifestation of the etiology of a disease. Even love itself is now the pathological expression of a lack resulting from the disease. Nothing I think is what I think it is because I am not in here; the disease is in here. All that I have ever been, or thought I had been, has only ever been that which conceals the ravages of the disease. And all expressions of myself are henceforth compiled in forms and files which track my disease. The writing of me is the writing of the disease. Physical symptoms, emotional tendencies, the kinds of things that make me laugh or cry, my moods—none of this is purely an expression of myself anymore. These are objects that are assigned to rigorously defined terms which fit into systems of understanding to which I have no access. For me to access these writings would be to contaminate and delegitimize them with my disease.

I had become a legal object which further stripped off parts of my living presence. The legal apparatus splintered me into myriad pieces. I was fractalized as the system identified, classified, and made determinations on my status as an object of legal proceedings. Even these legal proceedings split into multiple forms. The Law does not name so much as it labels. I was placed under a specific type of taxonomy which would determine my fitness for being in the world. The real term for adult probation, for example, is community control. Under community control I had to be evaluated regularly. My disposition on any given day. My ability to follow directions. My level of compliance with other court orders. I failed this on at least one occasion when the medical/psychiatric dimension of my being overrode my legal status. In other words, I showed up at my P.O.'s office drunk and was facing jail time for doing this. This notwithstanding my medical designation as chemically dependent. The two language systems operate according to different logics, different modes of making meaning, different ways of grasping what can and cannot be considered legitimate objects of understanding. They may overlap at times, but they are separate and autonomous systems. In any case, these language systems took precedence over any self-definition I may have indulged myself in retaining.

My "self" is also effaced and dispersed across the globe at the speed of light in the form of an electronic textual version of what remains of me. This text precedes me anywhere I go. Before I arrive in any physical sense, or, before any linguistic version of myself I may contrive to represent my physical self can be articulated—written—I am already there. The electronic brand affixed to my being is of greater significance than my physical being.

As I take up the problem of writing about my own "self," I am immediately confronted with the fact that the self I attempt to render into language has been splintered. Medical determinations which supersede a self as these medical systems classify my living body in terms that are intelligible to a system that does not include me, that absent myself from myself. There are legal language systems which are equally foreign and unintelligible to me and are designed to take control of my body and mind so as to correct me. There is the entire system of language that attends and underpins the diagnosis of the disease which further fractalizes into language systems that are medical, psychiatric, and even metaphysical. These further negate my living presence. Even before I type words intended to render experiences from memory into language that can be accessed by a reader, I am far removed from a self that is accessible and self-apparent. When I gave over to the end, I suicided the forms of understanding I mistook for my own.

To tie the fragments into a unified whole that resembles a tidy narrative is impossible. I do not have access to my own experience in the form of a direct narrative and therefore cannot recount these experiences in something so direct. The fragment is all I am able to provide since the fragment is what remains of my living presence. Blanchot's insistence on the fragment is enormous, and it partially depends in the belief that the process of rendering life into language is to approach a death in life. It is to negate what is fully itself with something that stands in for what is fully itself, and therefore it means to commend this full presence to death. To write the self is a suicide in these terms, and this leaves no self that can be rendered completely. Thus, the fragment provides a totality that stands in for the absence of a totality.

To allow myself to be re-written. My coming to be was a process of revision. Re-Vision with a vision granted me by the words of others.

The end is in the beginning

The end begins in my room. It is in the back of the building just over the diner where I work washing dishes and doing miscellaneous kitchen prep. It is a small room, roughly square although it may be slightly rectangular. I cannot remember for several reasons, not the least of which is that I largely lived my life in one side of the room. The wood floors are old and rough. They are dark brown with stains in random places. Toward the center of the room, though off to one side across from where I sleep, there is an old gas heater. It has to be lit with an electronic igniter that is so old it hardly works. It takes up considerable space. During the warm months I placed things on top of the heater like empty bottles and cans. Sometimes my ashtray would be placed on the heater in the rare times when I moved around the room such as pacing or simply getting up to move.

The contents of the room are sparse. I have a small couch, not quite long enough to stretch out completely. I sleep on this couch and my few waking hours spent in the room are spent sitting on the couch. I eat my meals on the couch. Mostly, I sit on the couch and drink and smoke. One wooden chair sits next to the couch which I mostly use as a table. I eat off the chair, place my bottles of vodka on it too (both half-gallon diluted vodka from the grocery store and 80 proof vodka from the liquor store). I also place my wine bottles there. My ashtray is almost always on this chair and always within reach of the couch so that I can use it both sitting and laying down. There are the shards of a plastic table strewn about the far side of the room. These are mostly over to the side I rarely use. The table was shattered when I fell on it as I fell off the couch. I do not remember when I did this. At the foot of the couch, and against the same wall as the couch, there is an old chest of drawers. I never use this except to put things on it. On top of the chest is a stereo system, the last remaining thing of any value I own.

Clothes are in piles. Some clean clothes are stacked on top of the chest of drawers. Dirty clothes are strewn in random places. There are plastic bags from the grocery and from cheap takeout. These all contain the remains of the food I brought back to the room and ate. I only ever ate in the room at night since I could eat in the diner during the day. Miscellaneous trash is also strewn around the room—bottles, cans, candy wrappers, odd pieces of paper. There are a few books that I still try to read, although I retain nothing of what I read. I have a moleskine journal that I still write in. The room has two windows: one above my head at one end of the couch, another behind the chest of drawers. The windows are never opened for fear of rats getting into the room. There is a long orange extension cord used to plug in an air conditioner to the diner on the first floor. This is done to prevent tripping a circuit breaker from the electricity load of the air conditioner which is still in a window behind the chest of drawers.

To the left of the couch if you face out, there is a bathroom. One step up from the wood floor. A shower to the left is peeling apart exposing the insulating materials behind the plastic. The exposed plastic is covered thick with mold. The peeling shower stall almost touches the body while showering. In the center of the bathroom is a sink, always filthy, with toothbrush and toothpaste on the sides. To the right there is a toilet, broken and permanently stained brown. This is a combination of shit and rust. The back of the toilet is broken and the pipes are exposed. One towel hangs on the wooden door to the bathroom.

It is here that the end began. Everything that ever happens in this room happens with me alone. No one ever comes to this room. No one ever joins me in anything I do here, and the only things I do here are eat (little), drink vodka and wine, and smoke. I do listen to music, classical music. In the room

I can hear some noise from the streets outside, but it is mostly silent. Being in the back I am largely insulated from the noise of the main street, and the alley behind is mostly silent. Junkies make their ways up and down, but they generally try not to draw attention to themselves.

I wake to the sound of banging under the floor. My head is a swamp—festering, bug infested cloud flies thick still dank water dry rank decay. Swinging my knees off the couch. Still in my clothes from the night before, the remains of a handle of 42-proof vodka (about a third full) and half a bottle of cheap white wine. Light up a cigarette. Drink (chug the last of the vodka and wine). Head into the toilet to piss. The bowl is brown. Piss stains everywhere. The floor, the seat, the rim of the bowl. The stinking shower wall peeling into a curl with mold. Sit back down and stare at the floor. Smoke. Brush my teeth and head into the cold air. I start filling the sinks and get coffee and water. Drink both. Wait. Throw everything up and dry heave for several minutes. My sinks are full. Sneak out the back door. I am wearing a t-shirt and my apron, it is cold, but I don't care. Quickly make my way to the Shell station around the corner by cutting through a parking lot and an alley. Make my way back with two Mike's Hard Lemonades, 8 percent alcohol. Crack open the first and chug nearly all of it. Light a cigarette. Wait. Feel my stomach refuse the drink. Hold onto it long enough for the alcohol to seep into my bloodstream. Throw up the lemonade. Dry heave for several minutes. Begin washing the morning's pots and pans. The dishes begin rolling in with breakfast business. Peel potatoes. Grate potatoes. Open my second hard lemonade. Chug it and wait. Throw up the lemonade.

After the lunch rush, I go get two more beers. These stay down. I make it through lunch. Clean up the aftermath, the pots from the steam table, the grill tools, the grease trap. I get paid 40 bucks plus what the servers tip me out. Some days, it can be 80 bucks. Head back up to my room and shower. By the time I am clean and heading out the door to the bar, I am starting to shake. The shakes come on fast. More than about a half hour between drinks and I will shake. Longer than that and it becomes uncontrollable.

Buy a pack of smokes at the corner store. Walk along Liberty Street. It is loud. Cars revving, honking horns, corner boys yell and stare at me. No one says anything to me. Passed the boarded-up store fronts, the other corner store, up the hill. The bar is empty. I order a brown ale and a double shot of bourbon. I feel the alcohol in my center. It radiates out to the rest of my body, filling me, making me myself. People come in. The same people every day. I talk, but I don't say anything. I am deluded. I think I am just like them. I am not. I am not like anyone. I am alone. I drink—probably six beers and eight shots. I head down the hill and stop at the other bar. No one there. The bartender looks at me, and I can see the forced smile as she sees not a bar patron, but a broken thing, an old drunk; so common, so worn and uninteresting—a cliché. I drink two more beers and shots. Cut through the side street to the grocery. Loud, yelling, kids everywhere, people yelling at each other. The duty cop looks at me and watches me. I buy some fried chicken, a handle of 42-proof vodka, and a cheap bottle of white wine. On my way home the street is silent. Trash blows across the street and piles against the Franciscan building. I stop and look at the old architecture wishing I was one of them—a brother safe inside, close to God. I am far from God, and I know it.

My building smells like weed. Roy stands in the doorway to sell weed and looks at me like I am stupid, the way you look at a stray ugly dog. Up the stairs. Eat a little. Wait. Take long drinks from the vodka. I may or may not throw up.

Drink some wine. Smoke. Lay on the couch. Sometimes I cry. Sometimes I just lay there and stare. Smoking. Drinking. Long drinks from the vodka bottle. One night, I strung an extension cord over the door to the bathroom. Tied one end to the furnace and the other end to my neck. I hung for a few seconds but fell off the door. I think that is when I broke the table. I can't remember.

The impossibility of the end is that it cannot be. We cannot know the end because to know necessarily means we have not reached the end. But the present condition, so completely evacuated of anything that can be narrated, that can be placed in a narrative, devoid of the actions of one who acts in the manner of a subject that acts on an object. This is a subject that does nothing more than act within the infinitive verb. It breathes, it sleeps, it wakes, it eats, it shits, it drinks, it vomits, and it does it all again. Stripped down to movements that are not its own, engaging the various systems of the body that facilitate the things it does until one day, at some unknown and unknowable moment, actions, movement, thought (what little is left) simply ceases and the end finally comes. As Beckett says, "there is nothing more real than nothing," and this nothing is the everything that fills these vestiges of living. It has been said that we die because we cannot remember the beginning to the end. But this is in reference to a very real end, one that is not happening in this room, but one which I appear to have entered since I cannot remember a beginning or an end. And here it ended, but in saying this, the end would come to mean more than I can even fully describe to this day. What is considered living, the individual who lives, moves, acts in the world, is a vast textile of stories, some of the past, some made up of speculations of what is to come, even if some of these speculations are little more than the certainty that we will again wake up in the morning. Life also consists of a vast collection of articles of faith. That which we believe we are entitled based on what we have already done, is one example. I am entitled to return to work tomorrow because I worked today, what is more, I am expected to return to work tomorrow therefore the certainty of a future that holds a return to work remains present. The point is that there is never really an end until you reach the end, at which point there is nothing. The nothing is where I am at this moment. Where I was in that room. Even after my time in the room, the next present moment offered little more than a clearer awakening of my end. Yet, what came after was a dull sense that I would go on… to something I knew not what. Leaving the room one day to a medical facility that would help me through a medical detox so I did not risk seizures or other potentially fatal consequences of profound alcohol detox, I found myself in a place from which I never thought I would escape. At first, I did not want to escape. Then, I did not think it was possible to escape. But in those first moments, days, weeks—it does not really matter, and I cannot remember anyway, I saw clearly my end, and I was nothing.

It was not a moment, a time, a period of life—this end, this place, space, and time was a condition without name. It was the space of a disaster. I did not operate of my own will because I had abdicated my will long ago, long before the time and place that I am describing. And none of this can be properly put into language since it all takes place outside that which is accessible to language. Rendered without will, passive, subject to what may come, and nothing comes. This is a kind of passivity that does not engage my ego nor am I passive in relation to something other than myself. Passivity in the manner of the middle voice in which I neither act nor am I acted upon: "Passivity is measureless: for it exceeds being; it is being when being is worn down past the nub—passivity of a past which has never been, come back again. It is the disaster defined" (Blanchot, *The Writing of the Disaster*, 17). Stories only make sense when they are situated within other stories. Or, what amounts to the same thing, we grasp a story only because it fits within the larger collection of narratives that constitute the only Real we can know. My end is a condition that takes place outside of stories, outside of what can be narrated.

and yet
you go on

It was late fall. I woke up on the sidewalk in front of the building of the diner where my room was. I don't know what time it was, but it was late, dark. I do not remember being cold. As soon as I moved, I felt pain like I had been hit in the nose hard. My neighbor walked by and looked down at me. Without stopping he said are you alright. I muttered a yes as he walked away and into the building. I tried to move but couldn't. I laid there for some time. I felt a tightness on my face which I would later discover was dried blood all over my face. A younger man, maybe about 30, leaned down to me and asked for some money. I don't know why, but I pulled the wad of cash I had out of my pocket. The man grabbed it from my hands and ran down the street. I could hear his steps fading away. It was over 250 dollars. I was going to pay off my fines and fees to get off probation. Eventually, I got up off the ground and made my way into the building and to my room. My face was covered with dried blood. It was all over my ears. I must have passed out again.

I know I worked the next day. People staring at my swollen face with looks of pity, fear, and resignation. Even after cleaning up, I kept finding spots of dried blood on my face, ears, and head. That night I woke up in tremendous pain and could not get a full breath. I called 911 and the EMTs took me to the emergency room. I had broken my skull, flared it out like a spider web just above my nose. I also fractured a rib completely in half, and I had bitten through my lower lip. The nurses discharged me with the looks you give people who are on an inevitable path to killing themselves.

A few days later another neighbor told me I had fallen down the iron stairs face-first. I fell on him too, and he was mad at me about it all. I lied to people and told them I had been mugged. Got drunk and tried to forget. It did not matter much anyway.

3

It is hot in here. Early September still clinging to summer's heat, and the heat amplifies in the stillness of this room no matter how large the room may be. Dank air loaded with humidity. Few people in view. Just some counselors who play dominoes at a table near the main desk. The tables are arranged in rows of three down each side of the room. Long wooden tables made of dark wood. These would be beautiful in a different context. Here, these tables look like the furniture you would see in an old movie that takes place in a prison visiting room. Cheap metal chairs with torn vinyl upholstered seats surround each table. The walls are covered with posters that proclaim slogans from Alcoholics Anonymous, or they have quotations designed to either inspire hope or fear. Some warn of the dangers of relapse, others offer words of encouragement that have the feel of cheap greeting cards complete with images of oceans and skies. There is a large wooden sign above my head that illustrates the various programs available at the House. I hear the men slap dominoes on the wooden table and yell. The desk man grows angry from the interruptions. No one looks at me. I am invisible, or of no consequence, which amounts to the same thing as being invisible. Other than the sound of dominoes and chairs scraping against the wood floor, it is silent in here. I sit and I am numb. I am completely numb.

Regret is the only thing that makes its way to conscious thought. All the things that made me what I thought I was ended. Everything has ended, and there is nothing I can grasp that resembles hope, much less an idea of what may come even as early as tomorrow. One day at a time, they tell me. But regret seems to hold consistency even if there is no object on which to focus the regret. At this moment, in this place, regret compels me only insofar as it is made of the substance of thought which can only emanate from a conscious being. I do not regret any "things", I simply regret. "Regretting, that's what helps you on, that's what gets you towards the end of the world, regretting what was, it's not the same thing, yes, it's the same, you don't know, what's happening, what's happened, perhaps it's the same, the same regrets, that's what transports you, towards the end of regretting" (*The Unnamable*, 371). Toward the end and it is not the same; it is not the same as anything that has ever been. This regret is the final regret except that it is not the final regret. More regret will come as memories and full moments of my personal life history come into focus and even those things I once recalled with great pride and delight become occluded by this overarching narrative of what leads to this type of regret. Regret is what is left at the end of it all. It shatters or compounds in an endless fractalization, self-begetting angles, each singular regret makes contact with another and folds on itself to form new facets so that what was once a clearly demarcated and bounded system of memory and narrative flow is now an infinitely unfolding yet enclosed space of regret. To choose a particular is arbitrary and therefore pointless since no single point in the system of lines can ever offer a point of purchase toward mastery. It masters me so that "I" do not regret, "It" regrets in the same way that "It" is raining, or "It" is cold. I am at the point where all subjective flows have ceased and regret remains. I lived beyond the end of my own life even as I am confronted with something else which, although utterly foreign and not mine, is a life I am now forced to live. And so I go on filling a space offered to me that I neither recognize nor want. My things are emptied from my bag and transferred to a plastic garbage bag to be cooked in a hotbox in order to prevent bedbugs. I, say I, am where I am, in a place that is removed from places—this place is located in a specific geographical site within the larger site that is the city. But it is a place—a space—that is set apart from the rest of the geographically understood spaces that make up the city. This space is outside what we designate as spaces in which people live, work, play, worship, etc. It is a space within spaces, or a space outside spaces. The House is a space in the common way we mean this word. It occupies a physical place in the geography of the city and neighborhood in which it exists. But it is also a space designed to function exterior to social and cultural space. What is more, this space is external to the life of ordinary people who constitute the life of the city spaces. This space, where my "I" entered, transformed me as just one more individual among all individuals who constitute the civic life of the city into something other than the rest. The space I entered exists within the city but its status as a space is other than all other spaces within the city. This "House" is not one in which families live and create life. It is a space of crisis. This space is dedicated to a certain form of not living at all. Whereas all other spaces within any city serve a function that is directly connected to some other space within the city, for example, the school is directly connected to the houses where the school children live, and to the social and civic spheres for which they are being conditioned, the space I entered is specifically designed to cut itself off from everything else. Ours is a non-space within all spaces. It is the space where crisis can be free to unfold not necessarily for the safety and benefit of those who experience crisis, but rather, to protect the rest of the city from all of us who constitute the moment and pathology of crisis. This is a space in which everyone is transient, indigent, at varying stages of decomposition.

This is a place of exile. It is a space in the manner of what Foucault describes as a heterotopia. This place is both here and not here. It is a space of crisis, one in which all the other spaces of society and culture "are simultaneously represented, contested, and inverted". This place is a heterotopia, and might be described as a "crisis heterotopia". It is one of those "privileged or sacred or forbidden places, reserved for individuals who are, in relation to society and to the human environment in which they live, in a state of crisis". And yet, unlike the crisis heterotopias Foucault describes in which certain individuals are going through a ritualized period of life, this place is a place of crisis because we are individuals who are in a state of crisis and our current state presents a crisis to society in general. We are people who have lost control. Many of us have committed crimes, some of these crimes are serious. There are men here who have killed and raped. There are men who have committed crimes that are unspeakable. But we all present a danger to ourselves and everyone around us. This space, this house of "recovery," exists for us to exist alongside of society while we are both treated for our disease and are prevented from doing further harm.

Unlike heterotopias that are reserved from those in a state of spiritual suspension like a monastery, for example, this heterotopia is one reserved for individuals who require control, who have stepped beyond the limits of transgression on multiple fronts and at multiple levels. Foucault describes places such as these, such as the one where I found myself, as one of the "heterotopias of deviation: those in which individuals whose behavior is deviant in relation to the required mean or norm are placed." We in the House have deviated and are by definition deviants—abnormals, no matter the well-intentioned language now used to define the addicted. We know, everyone knows, that we are abnormal and are relegated to a certain type of space whereby our deviations can be corrected and reformed. Therefore, this place exists as a kind of officially designated absence. It is an empty space within the accepted and socially and culturally recognized space that forms the larger space that is the city.

A place like the House is designed to facilitate recovery

from addiction, but it is absolutely crucial to recognize that the methods for recovery are not universal. There is a specific program of recovery at this House. As a space of crisis, we must consider that the way we are understood within this crisis is to be rendered in specific kinds of language and specific forms of knowledge. Within the confines of the House we are all considered fundamentally equal. We are equalized by our pathology and our pathology is the only thing that matters. No matter what roles we once held in life, no matter our previous distinctions and designations, we become the same in the House. We become anonymous, blank, absent even to ourselves. Outside the House we are all known and understood and named in different terms and different forms of knowledge. But the split between outside and inside is complete. Once within this House, whatever we were or are outside is completely irrelevant. We can be treated severely for attempting to exert any markers of being external to our pathology. Such an act is considered detrimental to an atmosphere of recovery. To cling to past forms of social and cultural distinction is symptomatic of a self-centered ego. When I characterize the House as a heterotopia, I mean that we make up a community of people within the House that is analogous to other communities, but the internal logic and language of our self-definition within the House is completely insular and secret. Anonymity is paramount. Never discuss what goes on here to anyone outside. From outside, we are people who are to be avoided. At minimum, we are dangerous people who are driven by addiction, with all of the stigma attached to this. At worst, we are threats to order, decency, and life. And all of these perceptions of what we are can be true. Our world is a place within the greater network of places, but unlike others, we hide ourselves, and the communities beyond want us hidden, if not gone altogether. Thus, there is a schizoid quality to life once I cross into the House. I am never again the person I was, but I must learn to live, from within the discourses of the House, as one who "belongs" in the world beyond the House. But I must never lose sight of the fact that I am not like "normal people."

There are ritual components to entering this place. Having my things de-bugged and going through the list of regulations and rules; my mug, sheets, towel, toiletries—all the things I am given to maintain my hygiene including the rules regarding hygiene, are like a ritual of entry. It is at this moment that I am transformed from an autonomous subject in the world to a specific kind of being who is no longer completely free. I am not in control of myself, and I am here because I could no longer control myself. This moment of ritual entry into the House is one in which I come to occupy and begin the process of fully realizing my true nature. From my place in the world prior to my place in the House, I am made into a different species of being. I will live in a state of crisis within this space of crisis. Part of my nature, and the reason I must exist in a state of crisis, is that I am dangerous, and this is the reason for my state of exile. We are all in exile on multiple fronts. Over time I will begin to remember things, and as I do, I will see the logic in my exile because I will never remember anything as I once did before the end.

This heterotopia of deviation replaces the regimens of the everyday with regimens of its own design. Like the heterotopias of the city, the cemetery for instance, this place has all the trappings of the world but in an inverted form. While the commonplaces of the everyday world exist without a thought, the commonplaces of the House are given special emphasis. Personal hygiene needs to be regimented. Times of waking and going to sleep are regimented. Meals are regimented. Every care is taken to ensure that we, the inhabitants of this heterotopia, function like normal people because without this care and these regimens, we will function abnormally. The nature of being abnormal is that being abnormal is normal. We must be re-aligned with normal. We must be disciplined, to use another Foucauldian term and concept. Like the tree that has grown crooked, we must be yoked to the post to find our way to being straight trees ourselves. And we must never be allowed to forget that it is our most fundamental tendency, it is in our nature, to not be straight trees. Unless we learn to carry with us the rest of our lives the straight tree, we will fall to our crooked, abnormal, and deviant nature. The space of the heterotopia is designed to separate us from the world and to separate us from ourselves.

Unquestioning. Yet, there are endless questions. This, where I am, marks the end. They promise me that this is a beginning of a better life, one that is not filled with the terrors of the self. Myself, my selfish and self-centered self and all that, is now over and done and at an end. I can still see it. More will come as memories become refreshed, as memory itself becomes refreshed in the absence of new experience. "Memories are killing. So you must not think of certain things, of those that are dear to you, or rather you must think of them, for if you don't there is the danger of finding them, in your mind, little by little. That is to say, you must think of them for a while, a good while, every day several times a day, until they sink forever in the mud" (Beckett, *The Expelled*). This present tense is not yet experience.

[An empty present. The present is never really present. It is always a representation of an extremely recent past, and this representation is always contextualized by an uninterrupted flow of the narrative that is one's life. This seemingly infinite set of assumed relations and connections which suture one to a proper and stable sense of being in the world. The present tense I am describing is one that is disconnected in every conceivable way. It is a present dislodged from the entire narrative within which I understood myself to be in the world, and in the absence of anything that can give meaning to where I am in reality, this space outside of space, this crisis space cut off from everyday life, I am in a present tense that cannot be understood at all].

It is only what is at this moment, and it is clouded only with the feeling of the moment. I am in a murmur of an unnamable silence. "You think you are simply resting, the better to act when the time comes, or for no reason at all, and you soon find yourself powerless ever to do anything again" (*The Unnamable*, 291). Since at this point all will has been taken away which is why you are where you are, in this place with no real past other than occluded memories. Memories will begin to take on different meanings as you become aware, or are led to understand, that everything you remember is now a function of the disease that put you here. It is a disease of thought. Therefore, thinking is forbidden. My thoughts must be supplanted with a program of thoughts. The idea is that my thinking will become the thinking that keeps me sane. And so it was and is.

"They also gave me the low-down on God. They told me I depended on him, in the last analysis" (*The Unnamable*, 298). All that I thought previous to coming here consisted of the thoughts of a madman. Now that I am here, I am given the opportunity to not think my thoughts, to take on other thoughts which are those of a program of sanity, and to finally make these latter thoughts into my thoughts. I am also not I, which is to say, the I at the center of my diseased and insane thoughts was and is a delusion, a symptom of my insanity. One way I am to re-direct my attention and my thoughts is to rely on God, on him who I depend in the last analysis. What if I do not believe in God, I ask repeatedly like a madman. They tell me I will die if I do not believe in God. I make it a point to talk about God, to talk to God, to turn over my will and my life to God so that I may find serenity. And this is what happens once you are a madman. At least, I tried to believe, and by this I mean that I tried to believe that I needed to believe in God. This was one important way that my sense of self came up against things that caused me to splinter, to schiz. The problem here is manifold. I was told that I must believe in a program that insists that I believe in God in order to become sane. But I could not find it within myself to believe that the first step in this process was true. The fault here is mine, according to the program. I was unwilling to accept and surrender myself to both my disease and to God. Therefore, I was insane by at least two degrees. Yet, I learned the language of one who believes, but that really just made me an extremely dangerous madman, one who can appear sane but is not.

At the V.A. hospital, a man approaches me. He looks lost, confused. Mostly toothless and of an elderly but indeterminate age. Ball cap loose and sitting on top of his head rather than properly on his head. He clutches the Big Book close to his chest. I don't know why he approached me. He said he couldn't sleep last night. He held the book on his chest and God let him fall into a peaceful sleep. Then he walked away looking forlorn and confused. I thought, it is all just magic words. The words do not mean anything. They are like spells, a rabbit's foot, a crystal amulet—anything. Just magic words.

After the ritual at the desk in which my belongings are bagged up and sent to be de-bedbugged, the deskman explained how things work around here. I was given a mug with my name punched onto a plastic label (first name, last initial in the manner of AA anonymity). And I made my way down to Support Group that was already in progress. Shaking and wishing I were dead, I entered what would become my life.

Later that day I wrote the following in my journal:

> 9/4/13: Day one back in Prospect House. Getting ready for education. Deeply depressed. I cannot stop

thinking about my girls. I need to let go and trust that this is God's plan. Hopefully, it's the effects of the alcohol that has me so depressed.

If things go like the last time I should be Staged up by the end of October or the first week in November. Off restriction before; then I can find my children. The damage is done, but I can devote myself to being something of a father before they are grown. Do what I am told here. B__ got reunited with his son, I can do the same. Focus on recovery. Do what I am told, and maybe things will work out this time. Mourn the loss and get on with things.

"God's plan…" that is Alcoholics Anonymous language. I never believed it, but I was once desperate enough to try to believe it. Alcohol is a powerful depressant. With habitual and prolonged use alcohol can bring on suicidal despair that does not simply go away when you sober up. Coming into a treatment facility after years of heavy drinking that culminated in several months of extreme alcohol abuse, drinking around the clock, all of this had deteriorated my own mental state. The depression was only one part of the picture. I met people in recovery who had been diagnosed as bi-polar while they were drinking. Actively using a mind-altering substance makes anyone bi-polar. Virtually anyone who has had a blood alcohol level well above the legal determination for intoxication for a period of months is technically bi-polar. I was also living with the staggering facts of the current circumstances which had so destabilized me that I genuinely did not understand what was going on before my eyes. Diagnosing a mental illness in this state was superfluous. This is one of the reasons recovery from addiction is so difficult. Many people who become dependent upon drugs and alcohol fall into this problem precisely because they suffer with a mental illness. Many current theories of addiction suggest that all addiction is a symptom of another problem, whether it be mental illness or some form of emotional and mental struggle. Getting at the addiction part of the problem can be impossible when the addiction is an extremely complex fog that masks another deeply intractable problem. And what I was handed upon walking into recovery was God's plan. All I needed to do was speak the words of the Big Book, and I would find my way to God and to sanity.

I learned exactly how to be insane. The split for the madman happens when what he "is" no longer lines up with what he ought to be. In order to be sane, the madman must speak a system that is not himself but is believed to be the language system that will bring him in line with what he ought to be. I learned perfectly how to speak the system of what I ought to be, but I remained something else, and this something else became quite different than what I had been. This split, like all the others, became fractal—an ever-increasing complexity that even I did not know how to control. Am I sane in an insane place, or am I insane and believe I am sane? What do I make of this arbitrary step that enjoins me to seek sanity in a power greater than myself? And how do I negotiate this demand that I be something while I am absolutely certain that I am something else? Two selves emerge and split. Schizophrenia. I live a schizophrenic existence while sustaining in writing an existence that refuses to schiz. I find a path in words and language that are not my own, that preceded me, and thereby create an exterior form that occupies an interior space. The layers of deception begin to compound. I admit to others that I am insane, and I at least say out loud, and in front of witnesses, some of whom have the authority to testify to my sanity or insanity in official legal contexts, that I am insane. All the while, I operate and write in my journals the thoughts of a man who believes he is completely sane and caught in an insane place doing insane things. What I write in my journals are frequently the words of others that I have begun to substitute for my own words since my own words are tainted with memories I can no longer trust, and I find it increasingly difficult to trust my own words as being my own; too many of my own words have been revealed to be the words of others that I came to misrecognize as my own. And if I am always over there, in the words of others, I am never here where I am, and the words of others I now take for my own are as sufficient or more sufficient as any others—a madman, it would appear. What is more, I am surrounded by people who speak the language of madness. They claim to speak to God. Some of them take prescription medication to control their madness. Yet I am to accept that I am just as insane. I say one thing in the privacy of my own mind. I say other things in the context of the discourse of recovery and treatment. I say still other things when I am alone with others. And I feel alien even to myself, which would suggest that I am a madman in the last analysis.

II

A future is impossible, the past has become incoherent, the present, an inaccessible blank. All I had, all I could access were fictions, multiple layers of thought, and books I was not supposed to read since what I read led me astray from my path to God and sanity. Having the past shattered into a present that is meaningless, the future becomes nothing at all. What could there be, given the nature of all I had done, the nature of my guilt and infamy, the nature of where I am at this moment. This is a place that is not a place, a place removed from places so as to relegate these madmen to a space that can provisionally prevent them from hurting others more than they already have. This heterotopia of those who have so grievously abused their one sovereign freedom, that of the freedom of choice, to do nothing but injure the fabric of society at the level of family, at the level of our own children. We had become wild beasts, as Michel Foucault says, and we attacked the herds and families we should have been protecting. But Kings we certainly were not (*Abnormal*, 97).

We made our choice, and we are responsible for that choice. While decent men went to work and took care of their families. I, we, drank and obliterated our senses. Instead of nurturing, I became dangerous—to myself and everyone who came near me. I became abnormal. Like the heterotopic space, I am in a wholly different time. I am wholly other but also the same. I am, in the eyes that look in a mirror, the reflection of a grimace of monstrosity. The House, and life in the House, offer a time that is removed from the course of the world and a time and a place where I now belong, safe from hurting anyone anymore.

In coming into this place of exile and crisis, everything that went before was altered. Memories I carried with me for decades became different memories. Times I had idealized, times in my life in which I long believed I did beautiful things were now tinged with the features of my monstrosity. I have memories of walking through the woods of Vermont during fall. Mindlessly, or filled with intense thoughts. I could smell the leaves on the ground, the crispness of early fall as it struggled to hold onto the last of summer. For many years these memories were an internal testimony to a time in my life in which I changed everything. It was there that I began a process of becoming a scholar, an intellectual, a grown man with some kind of purpose. These memories come and go in fragments, some I am alone, others I am with various people who played important roles in the drama of memory. But the memories had been carefully preserved to bolster an ideal that I was different than I had been in the best possible ways. With the transformation at the threshold of the House, these memories became the memories of a deviant. Everything became retroactively redefined or deformed, and the walks in the woods of Vermont were entered into the ledger of symptoms of profound selfishness. This is how the process works. It has been noted that we do not really have access to memories of events, we can only recall memories of the last time we remembered. Memory is a replay of something that is always distorted by memory itself. The long process of recirculating the drama of walking the woods in Vermont had been refined into an ideal set of images. Each image carrying the metonymy of another ideal. The smell of the leaves on the ground made contact with a sense of myself that was itself idealized—the ideal ego in metonymic contact with a mental image to suture both the image and the ideal to an internal narrative that was insinuated into an ongoing narrative of increasing perfection. With the coming of the end, that entire textile of metonymy, narrative, and ideal were broken off, and what remained was never the same. Now the ideal would become attached to another ideal that watched over everything with the sneer of disapproval. The sneer of another ideal ego which contained standards of evaluation and condemnation. What I once took to be a simple and free flow of memory was now subject to an exterior ledger of evaluative standards.

The features of memory are always anchored by something external to the memory itself. A good memory, the quality of memory depends upon how it is anchored simply because the expanse of a moment is in fact a collection of random sensations and perceptions arranged after the fact into a cohesive narrative. In any given moment, I perceive smells, temperature, varying degrees of light, sensations on my skin. Pieces of information become lodged in my consciousness according to a context over which I have little or no control. I retain some pieces of information, some sensations, and I arrange them according to another set of codes over which I also have little or no control. Over time, these pieces of information and the narrative they come to form are refined and made relevant according to various points of identification—anchoring points. Every time I "remember," I further refine the pieces of information and the narrative. Then, a crisis point emerges, one that alters the anchoring point, and from this point on I can never recall things in the same way. All of these pieces of information and the narrative itself is detached and re-attached to an anchor over which I have little or no control.

Another way of talking about this is that memory exists in multiple forms. At minimum there are those memories that operate within the conscious freedom of recalling one's own history and which carry the semblance of truth. There are also those memories that recur according to an unconscious logic—a logic that is beyond my ability to regulate. Then, perhaps beyond all of these memory-bytes, there are those moments and events which cannot be properly narrated and are generally referred to as trauma. Memories repeat, traumas are repressed. In all cases, however, the value or weight of memory is determined from outside memory proper. Trauma exceeds the symbolic code that renders memory intelligible.

The present that was the end, culminating at the desk of the house in the Main Hall, I am in a state of indeterminate questions:

> Where now? Who now? Unquestioning. I, say I. Unbelieving. Questions, hypotheses, call them that. Keep going, going on, call that going, call that on. Can it be that one day, off it goes, that one day I simply stayed in, in where, instead of going out, in the old way, out to spend day and night as far away as possible, it wasn't far. Perhaps that is how it began. You think you are simply resting, the better to act when the time comes, or for no reason, and you find yourself powerless ever to do anything again. (*The Unnamable*, 291)

Any object of sense we may call the subject of the hypothesis. No theories at this stage. Not enough information is available to formulate a theory, which would be some kind of a potential explanation. At this point, explanation is a distant prospect. Everything remains at the level of pure speculation at best; it is a nebulous sense still under the realm of theory. Yet, it keeps going. I say it; it says I. It goes on; it calls whatever is happening at this moment going on. It is the end—of something. It goes on outside the will or desire of agency. There is no agency. Whatever it is, it goes on only as it goes on. Action is delinked from will. "I" appears only as a speculative (specter of) presence. I stand in for what I was in this moment in which I have lost myself. Carried along with a will that is not my own. As the systems of understanding on which my entire sense of self came undone, I became willing to allow other systems of being in the world to take over however much I did not believe them. And in allowing myself to become what I knew could not be true, I did not form a sense of self but a sense of the end of myself. The self of this end that is situated in the present tense of the House while the synchronic progression of life goes on without us. If we are in a heterotopic space, we are also in a heterochronic existence. We measure our time according to the 12 steps. These happen in their own time (in God's time is another phrase that is constantly repeated). We measure the days according to the schedule of the House. Wake-up is 6:30 AM. The door flies open, the lights come on, and a voice yells at us, "Breakfast time, time to get up!" We have minutes to make our beds and make them correctly because they will be inspected. We make our way to the Main Hall, get coffee, and smoke. Most often we smoke outside. Sometimes we go into a heated shed called the butt-hut. We all have assigned tasks. Cleaning bathrooms, hallways, stairways. We rush to do these things. Breakfast is at 7:00 AM. Boiled eggs, bacon, cereal… sometimes we get grits. I cannot eat the boiled eggs and give them away. I see guys save them. Rough Care is at 8:00 AM, but we are expected to be there at 7:50 AM. All start times indicate at least 10 minutes prior. No one tells you this, you find out by violating it and getting in trouble. Getting in trouble means being "written up," a formal record of your violation is sent to your counselor. Most guys in the House call it getting "wrote up." Rough Care is a half-hour of yelling, call and response, readings from books that offer spiritual bits of wisdom and guidance. Support group from 8:30 AM to 11:30 AM. A half-hour break. Lunch from 12:00-12:30. Spirituality from 1:00 to 2:00. Education from 2:30 to 5:00. Dinner at 5:30. On the van to an AA meeting somewhere in the city until about 10:00 at night. Lights out at 11:00 PM. Everyday. Our only awareness of time is given to us from outside us. We have no access to time other than as an imposed schedule, and every day is exactly the same. As a result, weeks bleed into each other. Months come and go. We notice the seasons, but even these are measured in terms defined by the House.

Like the space that exists both within and external to official space, time itself, in the House, is exempted from the time of the outside world. The passing of hours run together in the course of a day. The passing of weeks and months become imperceptible. Some days, minutes can slow to excruciating slogs of time that simply will not pass at all. Sitting through meetings, classes, and prescribed groups becomes insufferable as we are held hostage to the improvised agendas of people who speak with nothing to say. Time moves on different registers. The time where life happens, where no one waits or notices or even knows anything about the minuscule events that make up our lives in the House, this time goes on without us. Children grow, have birthdays, mature, become the people they inevitably become—this goes on in our absence. Friends who remained, forget, and move on with lives we once shared with them. The grand and inane drama of the world continues to reveal itself day in and day out through weeks and months. In the House, weeks and months bleed on, and we become… something… Individual days slide like the imperceptible creep of old glass that is revealed only by the ripples that appear after many years. Nothing happens even while things are happening until days become opaque and rippled like an old windowpane. And we see through ourselves with the same level of clarity.

Within this, there is the progression of recovery. This too is not our own. We do not decide how much time is enough time or how much time we need. The time of recovery is one that adheres to nothing but itself. Some of us move through the 12 steps quickly. Others labor over one step or another for months. The process begins in Stage I. This is a time of intensive treatment. We never leave the House in Stage I except as a group to AA meetings around the city. The time of Stage I is indeterminate. It is up to a counselor how long one will remain in Stage I. Days are measured out according to the schedule of treatment programs. These are insufferably boring, and hours can drag on. Some of these meetings and programs are excruciating to me. I was in Stage I for about two months. I knew one person who remained in Stage I for 11 months. There is a Stage II, but this does not alter the time of the House. It merely allows one to come and go to work so that we get a sense of time outside even as we are yoked to the time of the House. I never felt like I was in the time outside even as I participated in the world outside. I was always "in the House" no matter where I was in the world. It was like visiting another world, one where I did not belong, and I knew I had to return to the House at specific times or face consequences. The point is that the time of the House is its own form of progression independent of the time in which the rest of the world measures out its days and nights. Sometimes the time of the House links up, but mostly we are out of time. We are not a part of what is outside.

Time is for outside the House. Those of us who have jobs must adjust to the time of the world, but I never came to view the time of the world as my time. I was in that time as a foreign body. Something that dropped into synchrony and left as quickly as I came. I was subject to a timeclock, but I was never a part of the time of people who are not part of the House. With the marginal status of the space of crisis comes the marginal time of those who live in crisis. We always know that we need to withdraw ourselves for our own safety. Those who become careless and allow themselves to fall into the time and space of family, for example, are doomed. They never come back. Falling into this place and this time can be eternal.

When I entered the House, the progression of the time of life and the world were suspended. The imperceptible and moving process within which we are all embedded, which is in fact a conceptual metaphor since time itself is nothing but the experience of time, was halted. There were those inexorable lines of movement through which each of us were on a specific path like trains on individual rails. These were not stopped so much as they were frozen in place. Some of these paths would be forever lost. Others would resume but in an entirely new direction. Time was pushed aside for this space and time within space and time that is the House and what is to happen in the House. Once there, we are excused from the course of events that are the world. In many ways this was a profound relief. Once I was in this heterochronic existence I was safe. The machinations of bill collectors, of courts, of landlords, of employers, or other people—all of this was held at bay, and I was left alone. These things could reach me but only through the mediation of the House, and this mediation conferred upon me the special status conferred upon madmen and the sick. We remained objects of jurisdiction and the Law, but these forms of power were quite content to not dirty their hands if something like the House was willing to take us on. Like the ship of fools of medieval Europe, we were in our boat of exclusion, and we took on the status of those who had been touched. We had the qualities of magic that the insane and the diseased had in ancient times. Much of this magic still persists even if it has different terminology for our times. The aura of the touched is now called an etiology of the disease, and the etiology of the disease follows its own chronology outside the demands of the world beyond.

It was in this place out of places and time out of time, in a state of profound depression and desperation, that I latched onto anything I was given. I did not especially care about the truth of anything. All I wanted was to not be what I had been and to not be what I had become, which was nothing at all, but this meant I had to learn to live with not being at all. Learn to be someone other than myself so that I may come to be myself. We tend to understand the idea of the self as a unified thing. If asked who I am, I offer descriptive features of myself. These are pieces of an image that I cannot really pin down to a unified "thing." I am always a collection of pieces that only ever represent one feature or another. For a long time, I was a hard-drinking intellectual. There are plenty of examples from literary and intellectual history to choose for this ideal. Take your pick, I modeled myself after all of them in one way or another. But take notice that there is a fundamental alterity to this descriptive feature of myself. These examples are not me. My I is an other, a distant and unknowable unnamable other. The other dimension to a self is the story of the self. A self is a narrative. I am the collection of memories (stories, idealizations, secrets, hopes, nightmares) of events and ideas that lead to this moment. I choose one or another depending on what aspect of myself I need to put forward at any given moment. I am an intellectual in one context, a father in another, and an aging punk rocker in still another. And I take personal satisfaction in each of these so that I am an irresolvable amalgam of all of them. To tell the story, to recount the narrative of myself, I would choose events that define each of these dimensions to myself. The things I study and studied, the day one of my daughters was born, the night I saw the Damned in 1986—these are all stories within the larger story that is the self that I claim. Each of these stories necessarily has others to tell the same story in a different way. Their story will include me, but I may, and likely will, fade into the background as a lesser character. I am aware of this alterity to the stories that make up the narrative that is myself. But where it comes to the narrative that is myself, I am the primary author. Even those things and events that I cannot control are subject to my consciousness as to how they will play out in the narrative that is myself.

The being of a self is a function of a narrative that emanates from an inner space and an external space of alterity. The other to the self, the ability to narrate what is my own requires my ability to objectify my inner world into a set of events and ideas that can be linked together to form a coherent thread of meaning. This otherness extends to the others that make up the narrative that is my self. That I am also aware that I play a role in the narratives of others, and that the richness of meaning that renders my own narrative a real and present self rather than a simple fiction necessarily means that alterity is woven into the deepest regions of my self that comes to be known to me and to still others as a self and as a narrative. Yet, all of this remains my own. I do not consciously think any of these things as I go about being myself at any given moment. To think these things and to Be a self would constitute a form of schizophrenia, one that finds the other of myself fully present with the self that I am. I would be split—schizzed. This is what happens at the end, in this empty present.

But at this moment, in this place, it has been decided that I will jettison all that I believed to be myself and take on something completely other as a way of being a different kind of self. I must "surrender," and I must learn "acceptance." I am nothing without a complete abandonment of the very idea of a self to another thing that is a "higher power," and this higher power is to be "the God of my understanding." Even the language I speak in the course of the day must be the language of a system that is not only foreign to me, but also a language that is made up entirely of platitudes and clichés. Which is to say, prescribed terms; pre-scribed, pre-written, a text that already exists that I am to take into myself and transform into myself as if the writing emanates from within. I am to become what is written, as in "It is written…" I must pray every day to "be relieved of the bondage of self." All of this unfolds in the House as an unresolvable tension between the self that I formerly knew and the recovery script that teaches me to be a different kind of self that does not rely on a self. I became schizzed almost by definition. Some people are good at performing this. The world of recovery is filled with people who live this performance. They know they are performing, and they know that everyone else knows they are performing. It is as if the performance is for the benefit of those who have tacitly agreed to never acknowledge that this is a performance. Not that any of them really become the version of themselves that 12-step demands. But they find it easy to perform the version of a self that denies the existence of a self to the extent that they seem to forget that they are performing this script. What do we call a sane person who pretends to be insane for the amusement of people who play along with the lie? I could never achieve this level of quiescence. I performed the recovery version of myself, remained a fractured version of the self I thought I had been, and came to understand yet another self that was acutely aware of the fact that I was doing all of these things.

I learned how to speak the language of sanity, at least I made it look like I spoke such a language even as I went on with my insanity. Playing with fire by reading and thinking…

From my journal, October 22, 2013:

> "The absurd is born of this confrontation between the human need and the unreasonable silence of the world."
>
> "the absurd is sin without God."
>
> Albert Camus
>
> "pain is absurd because it exists, that's all…"
>
> Charles Bukowski

For Bukowski it is on the order of the mundane, just the baseline fact of life that everyone laments, and it is the source of the ubiquitous "why." The absurd is simply pain, and pain is absurd because it is as certain as death. There is nothing abstract about pain, and its presence and certainty render it absurd. We spend so much time trying to avoid it. We calculate and maneuver, we go to doctors, we question those we love, all in order to ensure that we won't break our bones, suffer painful illnesses, and have our hearts broken. All the while, one of the few constants and certainties are heartbreak and physical pain. The health nuts' bodies will fall apart. And the most beautiful people will get their hearts stomped on for no real reason.

But there is the absurd on the level at which we eat out our own hearts. Regret will get everyone. Guilt is the price we all pay for letting anyone love us. All of this is the absurd. It is absurd because we face this with nothing more than the most abstract idea that our crimes and recriminations are larger than ourselves;

that there is something like eternity to which our debts are to be paid and our guilt measured. The consolation found in Camus is that the eternal is nothing more than an abstraction. It has as much substance as our childhood fear of the dark. This is why sin without God is absurd. All our self-imposed suffering is pointless; not in the cynical sense, but in the sense that we are free to jettison that suffering, to simply evacuate ourselves of guilt and regret just like we evacuate ourselves of shit.

The unreasonable silence of the world is simply the bad infinity that begins where we end. Outside of me, everything goes on forever. The infinity I exist in is completely indifferent—deaf and blind to my very existence. None of this is sublime unless we make it sublime, and one really has to consider whether or not there is anything sublime if we take God out of the equation. I can allow myself to be overwhelmed by the infinite, or I can just dismiss it as a variable for my mental calculus of my existence.

All of this inevitably leads to the question of God. Do I believe? Sometimes yes. I at least subscribe to something spiritual. Other times I feel more in line with the pragmatists. In the absence of the metaphysical and transcendental, there is a material and pragmatic obligation to the social arrangements we are given. As much as I try to believe, and even occasionally convince myself that I do believe, I really do not believe in God in the way this program insists that I must. Does this mean that I am doomed to an alcoholic life and death?

> That infinite that constitutes the unreasonable silence of the world neither frightens me nor even interests me. I am not in awe of that silence. Looking at the losses and the damage, I just feel broken but indifferent. Disinterested at the least. I am neither committed to suicide nor life. Like Sisyphus, I am resolved to the fact that, though all I do is push the same rock up the same hill, I at least get to walk back down the hill each time the rock rolls down. And then I will die. I suppose I am committed to everything just long enough to get my rock up the hill.
>
> Given the existentialist proposition, I do not see any other way. I will remain open to any and all possibilities and eventualities. It is all just up to me, not God.

So much bombast for a man lost in an asylum on a hill in a shit midwestern city. The real problem in this is that everything I wrote is in complete contradiction to the central tenets of Alcoholics Anonymous and the direct mandates of the program of recovery in the House. Everything I wrote is heresy and the ravings of a madman intent on his own destruction.

Just a few days prior to writing the above journal entry I had to do Step 3 in my Stage I step work. AA involves Step 3, but there is an involved written process for Step 3 in the recovery program at the House. In the Big Book of Alcoholics Anonymous, Step 3 states: "Made a decision to turn our will and our lives over to the care of God *as we understood Him.*" The italics are in the text. We are told again and again that the success of our recovery depends entirely on our willingness and ability to perform this step. Most of the people I met or knew in recovery simply reached back to whatever Christian claptrap they had been fed as children. Few people had any understanding of something like the Bible. They pulled out memories of simple lessons they had picked up in their earliest years, and these child-like ideas of God became a childish understanding of a magical force that would make their lives better. I recall a new man in the House who had only been there for a few days. He found a quarter in the change slot of the soft drink machine and told me, "God is already working in my life!" He said it with a huge smile and vacant look in his eyes. Moments like this were not uncommon, and some version of this kind of thinking pervaded their general understandings of God. Meanwhile, I was writing heresies and creating evidence of my insanity. But I could talk to men like the one described. I did it all the time. I talked about "taking God with me" when I left to go look for a job. I spoke of God while I listed all the requisite features of my Step 3 written work. I gave a definition of God as I understood him in front of a room full of other struggling alcoholics and our recovery counselor. I could speak of God and convince others that I had turned my life and my will over to the care of God.

That step work required multiple entries that pertained to my ideas of God, what the God of my understanding really is, and there are right and wrong answers to these questions. There was no room for me, or anyone else, to engage in theological speculations, to enter into the vast complex history of the meaning of the divine, and certainly no room for a flat-out denial of the existence of God. Atheism = death in the 12-step world. So I cobbled together some ideas I thought would fly. I got through it, and the ideas I put forth that day became known as my official declaration of the God of my understanding. And as the journal entry appears to show, I tried to believe. I tried to say I believed long enough and with enough conviction that I thought I would come to believe in time. Another AA cliché is "fake it til you make it." I didn't really think I was faking anything. I sincerely thought that if I continued to tell myself and others that I believed in God that I would forget all my old doubts and misgivings and would come to believe in God.

On our way to the big new church that is in an old industrial building. The one with the free gourmet coffee and the big television monitors that tell you what the program/service is all about. The kids in the back seat. This was all her idea, and I was going along for the sake of peace. We needed to do something moral, she said. Find morality in this church, she believes, says she believes. The rage burning just below the surface. The children sit quietly in the back seat. They are used to these moments of calm before the mother explodes. I am dressed for church—nice pants instead of jeans, a shirt and a jacket, no tie, this is a contemporary church. They like to advertise that they are a church for people who do not like church. We exit the highway and approach the main road that will take us to the massive parking lot, and she begins. She lists all the ways I am a failure. Why I never succeed and cannot provide for the children. That look on her face of sickening hatred. The most sickening face I have ever seen. The children hear it all. Her condemnations, her hatred, her age-old list of my crimes and failures. Finally, as we approach the traffic light, she says it: "You make me sick!" We stop at the light. I get out of the car and walk away. I don't even care where I am or where I am going. All I am doing is walking away from her. Morality and church.

A few months after I did my third step, I stood in front of a group to read my answers to their questions as part of the program designed for relapse prevention. We are given about 20-30 questions that are alleged to address our "defects of character." One of my questions was about my understanding of God. I told the group, "Santa Claus God and Harry Potter spirituality are never going to work for me." This was the nail in the coffin of God and my understanding of God as far as 12-step was concerned. That guy who found the quarter in the soft drink machine can have that God. I am a madman. Giving up what I know to be true is giving up myself. But in doing this, I gain access to something else. "One of the ruses of the self: to sacrifice the empirical self the better to preserve a transcendental or formal I; to annihilate oneself in order to save one's soul (or knowledge, including un-knowledge)" (Blanchot, *The Writing of the Disaster*, 12). This is to give up the self in order to retain the essence of a kernel of the self. That moment in which I completely capitulated to the disaster, to the end, in which there was nothing left of all those narratives, connections, others that define a self, I came to a place in which I had only the most elemental self (which is to say, not a self at all but a passive and dissipated self)— this "end," as I have called it, is where that which remains begins to encounter the space in which the writing of a self from what is already written can begin. Moments of refusal did not constitute a moment in which I stood up for myself. Quite the contrary, these were moments of refusing the way of being that would become a new way of being myself. I told everyone "Nuts."

On the one hand I learned the language of recovery and regurgitated it as needed. On the other hand, a completely different space was carved out that came from outside of me. But in coming to this outside, I found, or maybe invented, my inside, my interior, my Self. The encounter with the words of others, no matter the conventional line on those words, became pieces of another self. While the language that was handed to me, indeed, the language that was to be my sole salvation and one true way to regaining my sanity, was always foreign to me, I found the language of others to be a space of being myself that relieved me of the self that I had buried and lost in the end. And rather than approach the language and words of others as I had in my former days, in the days that are now dead and gone, I scoured that language less like a scholar and more like a rat. Like Templeton the rat who found discarded words to save a pig, I took the words I wanted and needed as I found them, as they found me. I read what spoke my self. In essence, I deliberately read in the wrong ways. What was in those things I read amounted to a secret language meant only for me. Rather than read to find my way toward sanity, I read to swim downward into insanity, and in doing this, I found another way. "To write: to refuse to write—to write by way of this refusal. So it is that when he is asked for a few words, this alone suffices for a kind of exclusion to be decreed, as though he were being obliged to survive, to lend himself to life in order to continue dying" (Blanchot, 10). This is an exchange. I will give up—surrender—and in exchange I will be given, or I will create, a form of a self that is both new and an amalgam of what was, all of this detoured (detourned) into something unknowable in advance. Without ever being fully aware of what was happening, I found myself in the places where I am not. If the House provided a place removed from places and made it possible to insinuate myself into a temporal plane removed from the march of the world, the end, the disaster I encountered at my end dislocated my sense of myself to an extent where I met myself in the words of an other, of multiple others, and that "I, say I. Unbelieving. Questions, hypotheses, call them that" allowed me, made it possible for me, to go on, to "Keep going, going on, call that going, call that on. Can it be that one day, off it goes;" it being the I that is myself (*The Unnamable*, 291). Transformed into an impersonal other, I say I. Where was I casting but in the worlds created by others? Rather than read these things for understanding, much less mastery, I read to find something that created me before I got there. To tap that vibration that precedes language, that unnamable absence that is my own absence.

Even as the House built its culture out of ideals like fellowship and service to others, and even though I was told time and again that AA is a "we program" and I would never need to be alone again, I came to be increasingly and finally alienated and isolated. While I spoke the proper language of the program and the House, the speaker was never me. I was always elsewhere, and the longer this went on the more I came to realize that I really was not coming to be this way, I had always been this way. On November 9, 2013 I wrote: "I must do what I am told, but I will never be deluded by sheep again. I am forming a firm understanding of *dio boia*." The hangman god became a fine image for a monad in a world of bad dreams that make up the day to day of life. From *The Memoirs of Chateaubriand*: "This impossibility of length and duration in human relationships, this profound oblivion which follows us, the invincible silence which takes possession of our graves and spreads to our houses, brings me back time and again to the need for isolation."

From my journal, October 14, 2013:

> Tiny and monotonous, the world has shown—will always show us—what we are: oases of fear in the wasteland of ennui." Baudelaire quoted from "The Voyage." *The Insufferable Gaucho*. Roberto Bolaño.
>
> Bolaño talks about this further in his essay. What is striking first of all is Baudelaire's claim that the matrix

of life is the sea of ennui. Though the word is loaded, it basically means boredom. Life, the world, our world is a wasteland of boredom. Not just any boredom, but that life is boredom. And we are individual oases of fear. Here again, the term carries more weight than it first appears. An oasis is a pocket, a small space of respite and safety; even a small paradise. But we are not small individual pockets of safety; we are individual cases of fear. The baseline constitution of life is boredom and the only thing that interrupts the boredom is fear. Life is a tiny monotonous unfolding of dull rounds, over and over, interrupted by animalcules of fear.

I question Baudelaire on this, although I believe he is largely correct, For the majority of the herd, boredom is not only the condition of Being, the fear that defines the human is the fear of the loss of boredom. But most importantly, I wonder what happens when the fear starts to subside. Is this the symptom of death, of the death of our essence? Though the body may persist to eat, shit, and sleep, is the slackening of fear that defines me as an oasis in the wasteland of ennui indicate that I am fading away. Because desire is a symptom of fear, and I have no desire. It is the life engine that starts with the perceived loss of the primary object of demand. With a diminishing desire there must be a complementarity in the diminishing of fear. The attachment to that first object-cause has begun to lose its grip, and, though I persist as a biological fact, I have begun to return to the zero state.

Feeling the loss of myself as an objectal other from which I know myself, I found a lack of fear and a lack of desire. Therefore, the self cannot be supported except as an external self that is not mine. Yet, reconstituting myself somewhere else. In the words of others. Here, in the passage from my journal, I found it useful to believe that I was never properly oedipalized. I came from a place in which this simply never took hold, and this is quite possible given where and who I came from. But in this view of things, I could not exist to myself except insofar as I disavowed my existence, and what remained was something or someone outside me. This semi-delusion became (and remains) a comforting idea(l). This was a way to lend myself to life in order to continue dying, to paraphrase Blanchot. I learned to be as if I was not: I created a space somewhere else where the "I" could remove itself to an absence that is not compelled to speak, to enact what I am not: "(T)here I am the absentee again, it's his turn now, he who neither speaks nor listens, who has neither body nor soul, it's something else he has, he must have something, he must be somewhere, he is made of silence, there's a pretty analysis, he's in the silence" (*The Unnamable*, 413). That part that is me but not me, in the silence where I am not, the silence I am unable to keep.

In an old photograph we are all together. A black and white photograph. The mother to the left, father on the right. I am in there somewhere, but I cannot picture myself in the picture. The sibling to one side looking smug. Cheap suit, plastic clip-on tie. Smiles that could be grimaces. The nuclear family arranged as nuclear families are arranged. Each particular from someplace else, from other places and other families. All unrelated and unaffiliated, yet arrayed as a nuclear family should be arrayed in the nuclear world of nuclear bombs which the father believes are the salvation of this land and the mother remains quiet about. I can retrieve this image from my memory, but I have no memory of the moment in time. It is as foreign to me as any old photograph of nameless people from a nameless time. And I cannot remember myself in the image. I have no memory of the moment and no memory of the self in the image.

> Like light at nightfall. Stands there facing east. Blank pinpocked surface once white in shadow. Could once name them all. There was father. That grey void. There mother. That other. There together Smiling. Wedding day. There all three. That grey blot. There alone. He alone. So on. Not now. Forgotten. All gone so long. Gone. (Beckett, *A Piece of Monologue*)

That grey void in the photograph is the hole in my memory that is myself. And I could once name them all, but it is now forgotten but for the memory of an image of a moment in time that I have forgotten. This comes to me while recovering my memory with a clarity I had not known for decades. Clarity of memory gives rise to a re-configuration of memory. The elements remain the same, but these elements are now yoked to different structures of meaning, different logics of how meaning is made, new values and systems of importance. And what formerly could not be remembered often becomes the center of a memory. The way I spoke of memory above comes to the fore. While once I recounted stories from my childhood along with others who remembered their childhood, pooling memories for the sake of a laugh or for a shared time of sadness or grief. Now this memory, or lack of memory returns as that grey void that was my childhood. Buried in the wealth of things was the utter poverty of conjunction between people. And we were a family linked exclusively by conjunction. There were no blood-ties to us. I learned late in life that my sister shared this lack, and it made her angry. She died filled with a blind rage toward the mother and the father, numbed by Soma, Ativan, and Vicodin, accelerated with alcohol, in the hallway of her house one night, her daughter found her unresponsive. We were just grey blots, there alone together, all gone so long… gone.

Family Group: An exercise in silent endurance; a two-hour block defined, for me, by an ability to remain utterly detached while maintaining the appearance of not just interest but deep personal investment. Family Group meets once a week, on Saturday Afternoons. It attempts to link our own recovery in AA with the complementary program for the family members of alcoholics called Al-Anon. Family Group is well-intentioned insofar as we get to hear from the people who are struggling with their own form of recovery, one that is the direct result of people just like us. While we are licking our wounds and finding our way back to sanity, we get the opportunity to hear the stories of people who were deeply wounded by alcoholics like us. The problem with Family Group is that there is really no way of presenting this except as yet another one-hour stretch in which we are presented with the damning evidence of the vile things we did to our own families, our own children, our own wives, husbands, and parents. As much as it is presented as a form of co-recovery, it becomes a review of sins and transgressions that can never really be made right. We are bad people. We did terrible things. Here are people who had been victimized by people like us. There are sessions of Family Group that are presented as an opportunity to heal. And there are other sessions of Family Group that become a review of the vile things we did to others and the sickening aftermath.

Since this group depends on volunteers who come to the House for our benefit, it is always a crapshoot as to what we are in for. Most often, it is the same person. She is a meek and slight woman in her fifties. She has no personality. I doubt she speaks much to her own family, much less to a group of strangers. She appears to thoroughly lack imagination. I never doubted that she meant the best for us and all concerned, nor did I doubt that she had been through some terrible things. The unfortunate truth was that she was just mind-numbingly boring. However hard she tried, no matter her good intentions, she was, and Family Group was, a gray blot in the week. And so was I. It is not that I was closed off to Family Group. It was simply a case in which I found no point of identification with it. The ideas presented to me were irrelevant. I found no point of entry, and it found no point of entry in me.

To be absolutely bored while pretending to care while detaching at a level so deep that the very soul is encapsulated much like those viruses, pneumonia for example, that are surrounded by a microscopic shell that make it resistant to treatment. My soul as a virus. But then that is what it had always been—that grey blot. The one in the photo that cannot recall, the one who speaks of himself and cannot recall himself—itself. So long gone was it ever there? Was it ever present in the world? It all comes down to "staying where you are, dying, living, being born, unable to go forward or back, not knowing where you came from, or where you are, or where you're going" (*The Unnamable*, 370). This is what I am left with when I unravel it all in this place; in the House. When I pull back the forms of self that have accreted from habit, I find nothing underneath, and "habit is what chains the dog to his vomit." I am a blank in a blank space, in a present that is not present. In a space of non-relation to all that surrounds me.

> But awaiting—just as it is not related to the future any more than to an accessible past—is also the awaiting of awaiting, which does not situate us in a present, for "I" have always already awaited what I will always wait for: the immemorial, the unknown which has no present, and which I can no more remember than I can know whether I am forgetting the future—the future being my relation with what is coming, does not come and thus does not present, or re-present itself. (Blanchot, *The Writing of the Disaster*, 117)

The legal term for adult probation is "community control." When the criminal courts decide it is safe to let you into the world but not safe enough to allow you remain unsupervised in some capacity, they place you into a system that is designed to allow the "community" to observe your movements, your actions, your place of employment, your home, and your words. Since the community itself cannot watch you, nor does the vast majority of the community have any interest in you, there are designated officials who stand in for the community. These are specific types of police officers known as probation officers. They have all the authority of a cop on the beat, but they sit in cubicles in large offices and read computer screens which roll out the information that has been tabulated and compiled on those deemed to be in need of community control. The information in these computer files contain things like past criminal history, employment records, psychological profiles, medical history, education levels, home addresses and phone numbers, alternate phone numbers, and any other information that may allow the probation officer to make determinations regarding your fitness to walk free among law abiding citizens. It is entirely at the discretion of any given probation officer to determine if you should remain free or if you should be placed under greater control by having you taken into custody and incarcerated. The people who do these jobs are just cops. They have no special training in how to assess people, how to recognize individual struggles or problems. They are not interested in anyone's health or well-being. And they do not care if you are a good or a bad person. In fact, most of these people are not very intelligent. Police administrators deliberately screen out people who score too high on cognitive ability tests because people like that tend to bring judgment to bear on situations that pertain only to the law. These people blindly administer the mechanisms of community control. Their only job is to decide if you have met the requirements of community control, and this does not leave room for personal judgement. The law is simply a code, a script that rigorously defines specific terms and conditions. Those who administer the law are never meant to interpret the law. Interpretation requires judgment, intuition, knowledge of facts and conditions that are not specifically defined in the law. For this reason, probation officers, or any law enforcement officer for that matter, are not the least interested in contexts. They are functionaries, and, like all functionaries, they are not intelligent or insightful. They get these jobs precisely because they are not intelligent or insightful. Intelligence and insight would compromise their ability to do their jobs. The law and the reality of one's life never actually coincide. Thus, in the final analysis, while under community control, you cease to be a living human in the world and become the image of yourself that is created by the lists of information at the disposal of your probation officer. To be a physical presence generally means you have transgressed the written code and are subject to penalization. If the language systems of community control exist to render you incorporeal, you are best served by remaining that way.

Many of the guys at the House were there as a condition of the courts. Drug court, as it is called, sends men convicted of drug related offences to rehab in lieu of a prison sentence. The condition is that these men must successfully complete drug and alcohol rehab at which point they are free of their drug offences, many of which are felonies with lengthy jail terms. Heroin possession, for example, can land a person in prison for several years. Most of these guys were addicted to one drug or another and letting them seek drug treatment rather than putting them in prison is the best way to deal with them. Prison turns people into criminals, and many of the guys in the House were criminals only insofar as they were addicted to an illegal drug. I fit into to this because treatment for alcohol abuse was a condition of my probation, or community control—a condition I refused to meet for most of my time under community control. My decision to go into rehab was motivated by my own desire to stop drinking myself to death, but it had the added benefit of meeting the conditions of my community control sentence. But not before I violated that condition by showing up to my meeting with my probation officer drunk.

When I arrived at the House, I was facing a probation violation that could have gotten me sent to jail.

Sitting in the waiting room with all the others. My hands shaking so badly I had to sit on them. I was sick and getting sicker. It had only been about 12 hours since my last drink, but I was in bad shape. By the time she called me I was visibly shaking all over. I sat down across from her at the desk. She looked at her computer and typed in some information. Then she looked at me, "Have you been drinking." "No," I told her. She got up from the desk and walked toward the back of the room filled with cubicles. After a few minutes she came back with a breathalyzer. I had a BAC of .107, well over the legal limit to drive a car. After more than 12 hours, my blood alcohol level was still at the level of intoxicated. She began writing the citation for violating the conditions of my community control, I asked her if I was going to jail. She told me no, but I had to find someone who was not intoxicated to come collect me. I eventually got a friend on the phone. After about an hour, he showed up, and my probation officer let me go, my copy of the probation violation in my hand and a court date. I later found out that soon after I left, my probation officer told my friend I was killing myself. I left the building of the offices of community control, turned right onto Eighth Street, and made another right into a bar. I ordered a double well-vodka. I couldn't even pick it up. I had to sneak a straw from the bartender's supplies and drink the vodka with a straw. After this, I went to another bar and drank cheap vodka for the rest of the day.

I finally saw the judge one fine day. Amid some shouting to lock me up, the judge decided that I could go back to the House and see how treatment worked.

Community control becomes your identity. While we in the House prayed to God to be relieved of the burden of self, the courts were doing just that. I was a collection of documents, many of which survive to this day, that detailed who I was in rigorous language. These details are not important. What is important is that I existed in multiple forms. As I entered into the end, the disaster, my "self" faded from existence and was subsumed by a series of other selves that had more value than my physical being. The more the world before me contracted and became a function of this heterotopic in-between that is the House, the more other versions of me proliferated and took on importance. I seemed to disappear the more the writing about me abstracted myself from myself. The more was written about me, the less I existed in the flesh. My flesh simply never entered into the language that described me. Legal forms and the language of treatment and recovery became more real than I was, and I faded from existence in the face of the writing that took the place of me. Community control offered several versions of me, the House provided several more, what would eventually emerge in family court provided still more written versions of me. I became increasingly nothing. As I was named by Others, I became unnamable to myself. I came to exist in a place that is in between the world in which people live life and a no-place, and I increasingly came to exist even to myself within an in-between space, a space in which there is nothing to go back to and no reason to think there is anything to move toward. My "I" was positioned in a "fissure which would be constitutive of the self, or would reconstitute itself, but not as a cracked self" (Blanchot, *The Writing of the Disaster*, 78). I do not know what Blanchot means by the writing of the disaster, but I know what came to be after I came to my end.

It is important to recognize that things like community control, medical and psychiatric diagnoses, including the diagnosis of substance abuse disorder, and all other official records do not simply lay idle until they are needed for one reason or another. These documents and records take on a life. They replace a person's identity with an official identity that has little to nothing in common with one's personal identity. Many of these things are officially permanent, and even the ones that are alleged to be erased or expunged are never really gone. In these days of electronic monitoring and record keeping, the official designation of what a person "is," remains essentially eternal. These are the holy records of what you are and what you did. These are the divine designations of your mental and physical fitness. These are the brands burned on your electronic flesh. In place of the king and his royal body, there is the body of the community as it is represented by a system of laws and legal channels which intersect and twist around each other into an impenetrable knot of knowledge that is not your own. When I say that my "I" was replaced by the writing of a disaster, I mean just that, and the book that is my "I" will live beyond my physical death.

Stigmata were originally the brands on a slave to signify that that the slave's body was owned. It is Saint Paul who re-articulates the meaning of the term in the context of a holy reference. Paul tells his followers: "From now on, let no one make trouble for me; for I carry the marks of Jesus branded on my body" (Galatians 6.17). From this point on the brand on the body of a slave can take on a dimension which carries the force of a divine message. The signification of a mark on the body as testament to Christ is tied to Christ's appearance before the apostles after the crucifixion. When he appears before the disciples, they are afraid and take him to be an apparition. Christ reveals himself, and it is Thomas who doubts the validity of his physical presence. With this Christ tells him "Touch me and see" (Luke 24.39). He is commanded to touch and therefore see—read—the truth of the resurrection. A similar account takes place in John 24.39 as Christ tells Thomas to "Reach out your hand and put it in my side." The signs of Christ's suffering become the signs of a direct message from God. This is the holy message and the holy enigma on the body of Christ. From these biblical precedents Saint Francis of Assisi could be understood in 1274 as having experienced the grace of the holy stigmata. The wounds which mysteriously appeared on his hands and feet are interpreted to be signs of the wounds of Christ's passion on the cross. The expression of the divine through and on the body constitute the holy enigma of the stigmata.

Stigmata have always been treated even by believers as both sacred enigmas to be hidden away from sight and as dangerous omens to be protected. The stigmata are signs of grace, and they are highly suspicious events. Nevertheless, stigmata have remained a presence in the imagination of believers for centuries. To receive the stigmata is to be directly graced by the hand of God. One is given the gift of the sufferings of the Passion. What is more, the stigmata have always been an enigma. The signs appear, but the meaning of the signs is unknown. Some form of holy message is manifest in the stigmata, but the content of the message cannot properly be understood. To then describe, depict, or otherwise represent the stigmata is problematic. The process of representing the enigma of enigmas plunges us into a realm of impossible signifying relations.

The sign which is the stigmata has a multi-fold quality. First, it is an expression in and through the body. The "text" is the flesh, and stigmata are not written in any real sense in which we mean writing, unless we take the words of Christ into account, and we can "touch and see." Yet the stigmata do function as a textual artifact. They are signs containing the requisite components of signifier and signified. One gazes upon the stigmata and recognizes that there is a visible signifier for the textual event and there is necessarily an object or signified. But the precise features of the signified are unknown. We only know that they are present. The constituent features of the signified are on the order of a sublime message, one that is beyond understanding but one which can be discerned in some form. To this extent, the stigmata function according to the formula of sign, signifier, and signified.

The stigmata have been recast in the 21st century. It is now those textual traces that signify one's value, one's status as a valid participant in the world. Once we are branded with the digital stigmata, this trace, this mark precedes us everywhere we go. The textual markers that define me within the legal, medical, and psychological systems that named me when I reached my end are now more real than my physical body, and nothing I will ever do will ever render me, life, and my body as having more value than the textual systems that branded me with the digital stigmata. The digital stigmata are more indelible than those on the flesh. They cannot be covered with clothing; I cannot paint over them. The digital stigmata lifts the essence of my physical body and projects into a space that exists and does not exist; it is both real and imaginary. While the digital realm is purely a space of electronic connection, it is also the form of reality that precedes all others. No matter what I or others do to re-shape our lives, the digital marks that define us are always already in excess of us, and these digital marks move at the speed of light. I can achieve a great many things, and I can write the story of these things in a form that represents me. But over and above the documents I produce, over and above the textual documentation of what I do and have done, there is the digital stigmata that takes precedence over everything else. The digital stigmata splits humanity into the valid and the invalid. These are my brands, and my only recourse is to devise another set of marks, traces, and textual elements that are separate to those that give power to the stigmata. I can never directly oppose the stigmata. To find an existence separate and adjacent to who and what I am.

In the earliest days in the House, I read only what I was told to read: the Big Book, the 12&12, the Bible, etc. If I read anything else, I made it a point to read things that were escapist in some form, at least to me. I read Stephen King, Philip K. Dick, Charles Bukowski, Arthur Conan Doyle, anything really that diverted my thoughts from the nothing that otherwise occupied my days and nights. I eventually made my way to other things, but what came to matter, what came to occupy my imagination, were writers who created the image of my heart and mind in ways I could never have imagined. In one of my journals, I recorded a poem by Pessoa written in by one of his many other selves, Alvaro de Campos. It is called "English Song."

From my journal, January 2, 2015:

> "English Song"
> I broke with the sun and the stars. I let the world go.
> I went far and deep with the knapsack of things I know.
> I made the journey, bought the useless, found the indefinite,
> And my heart is the same as it was, a sky and a desert.
> I failed in what I was, in what I wanted, in what I discovered.
> I've no soul left for light to arouse or darkness to smother.
> I'm nothing but nausea, nothing but reverie, nothing but longing.
> I'm something very far removed, and I keep going
> Just because my I feels cozy and profoundly real,
> Stuck like a wad of spit to one of the world's wheels.
> (December 28, 1928)
>
> This is the expression of my heart and soul. I am reluctant to even comment on this poem because all that can be said is said in the poem. If anything in this poem requires explanation, then the reader cannot "get" the poem. It would be inaccessible.

I honestly do not know if I copied the poem out correctly, and I do not want to look it up to check it. The entire point of this entry is the precise equivalence between what I was, what I read, what I copied into a journal, and what I had to say about it all. As a dark and invisible double of all that had been written about me and became me, I came to write myself into something Other. Some years later I would read *The Book of Disquiet*, but I had not discovered this just yet.

I sat at the table facing the judge. They and their attorney sat at the table to my right. An older man stood to the right of the judge, a bailiff of some kind. The judge allowed her to address the court. She performed her role of aggrieved victim. Her attorney made the case that it is in the best interest of the children and everyone that I have no contact with the children and be stripped of my rights to see them or speak to them. The judge asked me my thoughts. I said I was in no position to fight anyone. He asked if these terms were acceptable to me. I said no, but that I was in no position to fight anyone. Later, after the judge made his decree, I sat in a cubicle, the attorney next to me, a functionary in front of us typing on a computer. I could see the file in the attorney's lap. It was open. There was I, in a manila legal folder. My being separated out into discreet bits of information in legal forms. There was I written out onto a set of documents that was more real than the shell of flesh in the chair to the right of the chair my shell sat in. She said something to me. I ignored her. Some small shred of defiance flaring up. I walked out onto the sidewalk and wandered aimlessly for a few minutes. I remember I was walking fast. One of only two times I shed tears during the time of my end. I called my counselor and told him I was completely alone. He told me I was "caught up in self-pity. Get back here." I walked to a bus stop, got on the #32, and headed back to the House. Not alive, really. The final snuff of the light that I had clung to of a life that was no more. "I failed in what I was, in what I wanted, in what I discovered./ I've no soul left for light to arouse or darkness to smother." But I went on. I can still see that attorney's face, and, in defiance of the principals of Alcoholics Anonymous, I will never forgive her for inflicting such damage for money.

Twelve-Step constantly drives the message of surrender— surrender to your disease and stop fighting. To surrender took on different meanings after I reached my end. I was never passive in the sense that I was a beaten dog who just took what he got. Passivity in this state took on a different meaning, one that provides a space in which I could move without being detected. There is passivity in which one is a willing slave or victim. And there is passivity in which one withdraws from action quite deliberately. I came to exist in the latter, and there is a form of liberation in this passivity grounded in withdrawal. This is the power of being anonymous, silent, invisible; this is the passivity in which whatever I would come to be was irrespective of anyone's ideas or expectations. No more would I exist in a world that moved with the momentum of a personal history or a connection to all that had gone before. By withdrawing into my end and my passivity of being signified only by all that was external to me, I effectively disappeared. My journals became the other to whom I addressed myself, and it was in these fragments of writing that I came to exist as something other than what I had been before the end.

I wrote several things during the time of my end. One project was quite extensive. It is lost now. It was called "The Chief of Birds." I have no record and little memory of what was in it. What matters is that I wrote it. I read and I wrote. My life became so contracted into that state of passivity that even as I increasingly ventured into the world, I became more real to myself the more I invented the fiction of myself. I committed that final and fragmentary suicide that is the writing of the end while living within the space of the end.

From my journal, July 26, 2014:

> "Freedom is nothing if it is not the freedom to live at the edge of limits where all comprehension breaks down." (Georges Bataille, *The Impossible*).
>
> This is where the rawness of life exists. At the edge where all comprehension breaks down. Absolutely all psychological mechanisms for making order and logic and sense fail. Not the sublime. There is no super-added thought or supersensible faculty. It *all* falls apart. This is the only real freedom. Everything else is temporary and local—contingent and therefore not freedom.

The place where nothing coheres, where everything is in a state of complete disruption and external to categories and forms, external to narrative and even words. In the silent vibrations that precede the word—those unknowable regions at the margins of language. "And yet I do not despair of one day sparing me, without going silent. And that day, I don't know why, I shall be able to go silent, and make an end, I know it. Yes, the hope is there, once again, of not making me, not losing me, of staying here, where I said I have always been, but I had to say something quick, of ending here, it would be wonderful" (*The Unnamable*, 302). This is the place to allow everything to become what is to be. Giving over to randomness—the accident. And forgetting the forms of what I had been. I remember piecing together quotations and nearly random reflections some of which were fiction. It included a dramatic dialogue and some formless prose poetry. "The Chief of Birds" was an attempt to write myself back into living and to write a dream of another self that was more alive than the self that simply existed in the House. It is for the best that it is lost.

Moving on to Stage II: washing dishes in a cheap bar that maintained the pretense of also being a restaurant. This was temporary, but it lasted long enough. The bar/restaurant was owned and operated by an old man who appeared to believe he was offering something like haute cuisine. Each plate went out with a cheap mini-muffin bought in bulk from a grocery store that he carefully sprinkled with powdered sugar. He took great care to sprinkle each mini-muffin with just the right amount of powdered sugar. His presence in the kitchen during lunch was all we saw of him. He never smiled, found only fault in what everyone in the kitchen was doing, and walked away at the end of lunch service counting cash. He was a miserly and mean old man who lived in a world of his own invention—a living cliché. The kitchen manager looked like a profoundly unhappy man, someone who never meant to be a restaurant lifer. He had the look of someone who may have had aspirations of being a movie star but who has now become sullied by years of smoking, bad food, and being beaten down by his own submissiveness. He ended everything he said with an uncomfortable pseudo-laugh, as if he regretted the fact that he had to say what he just said. The service staff were all women in their forties who looked like they had been beaten down by life. Their faces bore the traces of heartbreak, anger, and regret; the tragic reality of women who never had a chance and gambled on people who just did not care. I don't think a single one of these women ever said a word to me. I was happy to be an invisible nobody in the dish tank. I did not want to exist while I was in that place. The worst thing about the job was that it was nearly an exact reproduction of the situation I had left behind before coming to the House. The sinks even looked the same. But now I was bent over the sinks fully aware of myself.

There are those who will tell you that doing disgusting and degrading work for little pay is one of those things that makes you stronger, that we grow as a person by doing these kinds of things. All I remember feeling was an intense desire to be smaller and more invisible. And these kinds of jobs made me stronger only to the extent that it strengthened my belief that the exploiters of the world need to be done away with. I would have killed the owner of that restaurant. I would still kill him. The kitchen manager slogged his life away and learned to cover his words with a silly embarrassed laugh because of that man. Those women who waited tables, took the lewd and sickening looks and comments from vile people, those women wore that regret and sadness on their faces because of that man. "But Camier, beside himself with indignation, caught up the truncheon, sent the helmet flying with his boot and clubbed the defenseless skull with all his might, again and again, holding the truncheon with both hands. The howls ceased" (*Mercier and Camier*, 454). The terror of it all is that there are no howls. Not mine. Not theirs. No one howls. We trudge and grovel with our resentment, and for most, the embers of rage fade into hollow spaces that are filled with silly embarrassed laughter and sad sullen faces devoid of hope. Or, what amounts to the same thing, a reprieve at the end of a day to indulge recriminations and regrets. Some over drinks, others in silent solitude. For me, just an empty form.

One night, the owner of the restaurant told me I had to stand in the parking lot to help cars park for a big sporting event at the stadium down the street. He said he would pay me fifty dollars in cash. It snowed that night, and it was deathly cold. I stood at the end of the driveway of the parking lot waving a little flag to signal to drivers that they could pay to park. The lot filled with snow. The next day, the owner counted the cash and told me I did not fill the lot. He would put it down as hours on my paycheck. I swallowed my hatred and rage and left for the day. I finished my time at the temporary job. Humility is a major component of 12-step recovery. Humility… humiliation… emptiness.

Venturing out of the House and into the world of work necessarily meant venturing into the world that was left behind. Having been written out of existence, we nevertheless retain a physical body, one that is recognizable to everyone we had known before leaving the world. Work, riding the bus, walking around neighborhoods where we once lived, and seeing people we once knew—all of this brought about a complex set of thoughts and feelings. Being more than one person all at once in the eyes of another, in one's own eyes. Present and absent simultaneously—recognizing something in the look of another… I am the same. I will never be the same. I am not.

People are crowded into the front of the café. I have a list taped to the counter of those waiting for a table. They shift and fidget, looking toward me but trying not to make eye-contact. The café is full. Servers come and go. I am on the espresso machine and the counter all around me is cluttered with trays, teapots, dirty dishes and silverware. I hear the voices from the kitchen yelling "food up!" Servers come and go, in front of me, behind me. Someone sits at the end of the counter and begins asking me questions. I get them menus and take their drink order. The man with his daughter who come in every Saturday approaches the counter from the other side and she orders an herbal tea. I have hot water running into a paper cup while pouring coffee into a mug. Turning, check the iced tea urns, grind more coffee, a server asks me for a cappuccino. The manager yells across the back part of the counter about the wait list. Voices from the kitchen. People move back and forth. From the back of the café to the front and back again. A group stands to take a photo. From the back of the café, an old colleague emerges. She looks at me, and in a flash, I see happy recognition and nearly instantaneous acknowledgement of what is happening, and her expression alters slightly as she attempts to contain shock and embarrassment. And I "saying to myself he's better than he was better than yesterday less ugly less stupid less cruel less dirty less old less wretched and you saying to myself and you bad to worse bad to worse steadily" (*How it is*, 9). Later, as she and her daughter are leaving after having a mother/daughter tea, she looks at me with concern, and says, "I hope things get better for you." She means well, but what she wants is to unsee me, to un-know what she just saw and not know that this is happening. I know this, and she knows this. We both know that we want, more than anything, to not know this moment, and we know we will never forget this moment because it is the moment when we both know that it happened.

The main concern from our counselors and our sponsors is that we stay away from people, places, and things that might lead us to use again, to drink again, to shoot dope again. We sign out every time we leave the house, and we provide our counselors with a detailed weekly schedule of every place we are going and everyone we will be with for any length of time. For those of us who are no longer on restriction, that is to say, restricted to the House other than work or approved destinations like legal and medical appointments, we have a degree of freedom to spend time outside the House. I wandered and wandering allowed me to not be whatever was left of myself. Wandering with little idea of where I am going, and directed almost exclusively by chance and necessity, I became an identity-less figure. Walking was becoming something rather than being someone, becoming and writing myself again using the directions dictated by the small freedom I was granted, the desire paths that opened in the city, and the rhythms of chance. Being away from the House, I was nonetheless a creature of the House. At no point did I ever feel as though I was a part of the world beyond the House, and this created a paradox in that I was to some degree free of the House but also free of the world that moved within and around. I was no one, and I was nowhere. Because "no matter how well he came to know its neighborhoods and streets, it always left him with the feeling of being lost. Lost, not only in the city, but within himself as well. Each time he took a walk, he felt as though he were leaving himself behind, giving himself up to the movement of the streets, by reducing himself to a seeing eye, he was able to escape the obligation to think" (Auster, *City of Glass*, 4). It was not that the world through which I wandered became the source of a text I wrote in one form or another; it was that wandering became the text that unfolded as I wandered. Walking was/is the text, it is the writing of a being who could exist at the border of all that had been written in order to efface me. "Me" could become "he/it: at the border of writing; transparency, as such, opaque; bearing what inscribes it, effacing it, effacing itself in the inscription, effacement of the mark that marks it" (Blanchot, *The Step Not Beyond*, 6). It was through wandering that I discovered a way to be in between all that had written me and all that I could no longer write myself. Neither subject nor object, a form of self that could "have a relation to that which excludes itself from any relation and which nevertheless indicated itself as absolute only in the relative mode" (6). Relative only to that which existed entirely in a receding proximity. It is only in hindsight that I can put the correct terms together to account for what was happening, and hindsight was one of the things I lost when I came to the end.

he/it rides the van with the guys. We assemble in the hall and listen to the deskman explain how it is. The deskman explains: "You are going to an Alcoholics Anonymous meeting. When you get to the meeting, use the bathroom, get your coffee, sit down and shut up. You might learn something. You are all full of shit and you don't know nothing, so you do not need to say anything." He calls names partly as a role call and partly to assign us to a van (we take multiple vans on Saturday mornings to accommodate the number of men going to the meeting). We shuffle out to the vans and cram in tight. It is usually fairly quiet on Saturday mornings, but often the van rides are characterized by chatter and bitching. Down the hill, across the viaduct, up through the university area, arriving at the VA hospital. The meeting is dull. Men say things that are meant to be profound. A man gives his lead: a long speech that details "how it was, what happened, and what it is like now." We hear his tales of drunken and drug-fueled crimes and misdemeanors. We hear about the moment he could not go on and how he found his way to AA. And we hear about God and his spiritual experience. We hear the same things over and over again. he/it writes in the black journal, the small one he/it keeps hidden for meetings so that no one accuses he/it of not listening. he/it sits and daydreams and lets the mind wander in preparation for wandering. After the meeting and letting the van driver know he/it will be going on a pass from the House, he/it walks away from the VA hospital. Up the main busy road that leads toward the road back to the House, but veering to the right, toward another part of the city.

Afterwards, I walk up the hill from the VA Hospital. It is a short walk up the road that connects to another main road.

Taking a right turn by the laundromat, I head into an old part of the city, one that is filled with memories of other lives led by someone who is gone now, someone who no longer exists. "I had not set foot in this part of the city for a long time and it seemed greatly changed. Whole buildings had disappeared, the palings had changed position, and on all sides I saw, in great letters, the names of tradesman I had never seen before and would have been at a loss to pronounce" (Beckett, *The End*). Past the closed video store, the Indian grocery store, the Greek restaurant; down the hill where the houses get larger and more cloistered. Medical offices, condos, an historic mansion, generic box-like apartment buildings… University students are increasingly recognizable. The park to the left, the one that was once extremely dangerous, but who knows now… I can smell the artificial lake from the sidewalk; the smell of algae and dead fish. I approach the main intersection and pause. It matters little where I go or which direction I take. Not having a direction is the ideal.

The House grants us this limited freedom after a time—a time they determine according to criteria that are unknown to us. Depending on how we are progressing in treatment, we are granted a pass to leave on our own. Most guys spend the weekends with their families. I spend the weekends alone and wandering through parts of the city that once had meaning for me. This freedom can be revoked, and often is, at any time for any reason. We are compelled to sign out of the House with a specific destination and specific time when we will return. There are additional restrictions on passes. Often, we have to piss in a cup after we return to test for drugs. Men frequently test positive for drug use and are compelled to leave the House immediately. Freedoms within the world that is the House are both precious and highly provisional. I never took my pass without the feeling that something would be amiss once I returned. The feeling of guilt the House insinuates into your being is unshakeable.

The path through the woods by the lake is a shortcut up to the street where we are headed. It can be dangerous cutting through the woods at night, but we walk through with a false sense of security. Our leather biker jackets and Doc Martens are the signs to others that we are dangerous. Loaded with beer, we make our way up to King Street that runs between the main road into the entertainment district and the University. I was alive then. I had no thoughts beyond the present. This moment with friends during a time in which an open-ended sense of uncertainty was simultaneous with an open-ended future. There was a future, and we were making it.

Around the lake, on the side that used to lead to the path through the woods, I walk with her. I hate her, and she hates me. My feeling of disgust is weighted with the lingering effects of the previous night's alcohol. I am trapped. I have no future. I endure this moment until I can drink again and not hear her voice. It breaks my heart that the girls are in this cloud of resentment. There is no future, and I want no future.

I wander through the cemetery and take the longest of the three roads. On a cloudy and cold November morning, I witness a flock of crows in the trees over a desolate part of the cemetery. They caw and crow at my movements, but they seem to follow me as I progress along the roadway that leads to a different part of the cemetery. For an unmeasurable span of time, I feel the presence of the crows. It is a block of time that is suspended within time. It is an ellipsis: time within time, memory within memory. A kind of parenthetical span of time in which I no longer feel like a being in the world, like I have been freed from the bounds of the narrative that accompanies everything I think and do. Later, I would write about it all in the black journal. I end up at a café, one that

I used to frequent in a former life that I distantly remember. I scribble in my journal. I read a book—several books. Look out at the sky as I smoke cigarettes. There are mists of hope, hope that she will come into the café, hope that everything will just become something else, hope that I never become anything at all. It all ends and becomes "something else not known not said whence preparatives sudden series subject object subject object quick succession and away" (*How it is*, 11). I wrote of the day's wanderings in a journal.

The times spent walking were of a piece with the time spent writing. Walking, I narrated my existence to myself. I often talked to myself out loud without being aware of it. I came to embrace my detachment from the world and from other people. Having found few meaningful connections within the House, I had little interest in making connections with anyone who still existed in the world. The world of common life became foreign to me, and I treated it with a provincial suspicion that was positively jingoistic. I disliked those who retained their ordinary lives and saw them with contempt. A reverse snobbery, you might say. The longer I remained in the House, the less interest I had in ordinary (normal) life, "for it seemed to me my eyes were not completely spent, thanks perhaps to the dark glasses my tutor had given me. He had given me the *Ethics* of Geulincx" (*The End*). Talking to myself out loud was a way of rehearsing my thoughts in the absence of a living presence. Walking, talking to myself, allowing my thoughts to wander as I wandered—these were the only freedoms I had, and they became the only freedoms I wanted. And in walking I was able to enact those things that gave voice to the separation that was life, the space of separation the House creates by making you part of the House. That primordial separation that occurred the first day in the hall and at the desk in which I became tethered to another mode of being that is not my own, but which made me aware that everything I ever believed was my own was not. I was never anything other than a tenuous collection of voices, of textual traces taken into myself and misrecognized as a self. What I read was no longer an image with which I identified. What I read became what I am, and all that I wrote became my interlocutor. I wrote to speak to an other, and I read to understand who was speaking. "This does not mean that he reads more gladly what makes him want to write—to write without desire belongs to patience, the passivity of writing—but rather that he reads more willingly what inflames writing…" (Blanchot, *The Writing of the Disaster*, 44). Nullified, I became something else and no longer cared to understand what that something else was, is, or will be. Walking, reading, and writing all became one continuous action. My "self," a nomad. My place, the space between what I read, where I walked, and the "infinite conversation" with myself. In some distant way, everything finally depended upon the *Ethics* of Geulincx: "*Ubi nihil vales, ibi nhil velis* [Wherein you have no power, therein you should not will]." But within the space around which one has no power, one finds the space to wander without purpose and from what one reads, write the fantasia of what one is becoming. Always becoming, because to be is under the authority of the Other. There was never a destination. The goal was to forget entirely the possibility of destination, I longed to be purely in a state of movement, of not being in place. All places had become a source of vexation either by the relentless killing of memory or by the trap of emplacement, of being held by something—anything. To be unknown (and not knowable) and to not know, these were the objectives, but also to allow all objectives to fade; to efface objectives so as to become object-less. And in becoming object-less, becoming subject-less. To be nothing but surface affect without ever falling into or becoming—allowing myself to be captured by or as an effect… "*an effect of non-effect*" (Blanchot, *The Infinite Conversation*, 305).

> you are there somewhere alive somewhere vast stretch of time then it's over you are there no more alive no more then again you are there again alive again it wasn't over an error you begin again all over more or less in the same place or in another as when another image above in the light. (*How it is*, 22)

Thus, begin again. There was what seemed a vast stretch of time. It was not so long, but in the duration it seemed vast, interminable, as if there could be no end for my end, and there could be no point of departure from which to begin again. And I have to wonder if to begin again is accurate. Does one ever begin again while life remains? But something like a beginning must have occurred in the midst of what was happening. A beginning that began in the same place. Is this the eternal return, to continually reach the future only to find whatever is left of the self that already was, that now is, and is never really present?

Being out of the House, working, going out on pass, even the stops at the grocery store after meetings, all of this inevitably means being confronted by the people we once knew in our previous lives. In these chance encounters I was compelled to face professional relationships that were damaged or even destroyed. The faces of those I once called colleagues or even friends within a world that demanded so much more than I gave. Even when I made it seem that I was giving, I was lying because everything I did was threaded through with the spiraling demon that would overtake all of me and become all that is left of me. I encountered old friends, people I had known for decades and had known me as I went through the transformations that maturity and experience subjected us all to. I knew that they knew... They knew that I knew... And there was a gulf between what they knew and what I knew. The denial of addiction is so well-known as to be a cliché. While I was revealing myself more and more with each span of time, they were watching me become other; they were watching as the façade of the person they thought they knew became increasingly pathetic, sad, sick, dangerous even. I was moving through it all with the signature features of addiction denial. If only I could get a job, a decent apartment. If only I had a car. If only I had more money. If only... It was always something other than me that was at the heart of all that was wrong, when the reality was that I was creating a living dung heap all around me. Everyone saw it but me. Now, after the end, after being confronted with the truth, or some version of the truth, of all that happened, I am now confronted with the witnesses. I see the looks on their faces, and these looks can reveal everything from disdain to sympathy to pity to an obvious desire to never look at me again.

For many people who come into drug and alcohol treatment, the drugs and/or alcohol can often be just one problem among many. In a great many cases, addiction is co-morbid with mental illness. This can be a widening gyre of struggles, one that is nearly intractable as people try to find the source of the problem. Is it the mental illness that leads to addiction, or has the addiction so contorted a person's psyche that they have become mentally ill? For people with access to the leading treatments in addiction and mental illness, the treatments can provide some measure of stability, although one needs to wonder if this stability has more to do with the economic privilege such people already possess and less to do with the belief that either the mental illness has been properly addressed or the addiction properly overcome. I have profound doubts that anything is "cured" since what we now call a cure is little more than a pharmaceutical patch on a set of symptoms. For those of us who are at the bottom rungs, those of us who have no resources, those of us who find ourselves in a treatment facility specifically meant for the "indigent," there are no resources at all for the mentally ill. We are given the 12 steps, and if we do not find our way to salvation through the 12 steps, then we did not work the steps. I cannot even begin to remember how many times we were told of those who "relapsed" (that term alone conjures a world of questions and problems), this meant that we did not, as the Big Book says, "thoroughly follow our steps." It was always us who came up short, never the treatment program. People who had been sober for more than a decade came to the House (or back to the House) because they did not thoroughly follow the steps. For the men I knew who lived with mental illness, there were no steps anywhere that could lead them out of their individual hells. There is no spiritual path out of schizophrenia. The presence of the mentally ill, the addicted, and in some cases, the plain sociopathic, meant that the House became something most people prefer to believe no longer exists. This space out of spaces that operates in a time out of time could be "the closed space where dwell side by side the insane, the debauched, the heretical, and the disorderly—a sort of murmuring emptiness at the heart of the world, a vague menace from which reason defends itself with the high walls that symbolize the refusal of all dialogue" (Blanchot, *The Infinite Conversation*, 198). Blanchot's summary of Foucault's Great Confinement is a good reminder that no matter our apparent enlightened views of addiction and mental illness, some of the age-old prejudices remain firm.

Thomas was not a big guy. He was a little overweight, and his hair made his head look like a cube. Still, Thomas did not lack a certain amount of confidence, and he was never one to remain silent about things. I remember him walking around in the course of a day with something like a childish smile on his face, as if he was up to something or thought you were. He came to the House through the drug courts. And he was a heroin addict. He was like all the others, sent to do a year in lieu of conviction for felony drug offenses. I think he had a few more charges he was also dealing with. Thomas had difficulties towing the line. He had frequent run-ins with the deskmen, and this got him on restriction again and again. Thomas always blamed the deskmen for this. Once he referred to the deskmen and the counselors as "cops." Thomas simply had difficulty working through anything that he perceived as standing in his way, and he went about this in childish ways. No one told us, but Thomas was also schizophrenic. He took prescribed medication for his illness, but the medication did not "cure" him of schizophrenia. A guy like Thomas needed medication and an intensive program of psychiatric care. He just could not control himself. No one had any real problems with Thomas. It was more a matter of Thomas complicating the program in the House for himself. He was doomed to failure, and I knew he would never make it through his year.

After Thomas was told to leave, I lost track of what became of him. Word made its way back to us that Thomas was still caught up in the court and legal system. One day, we found out Thomas was in prison in another state. I never found out what that was about. I only knew of his local legal troubles. In a short time, I largely stopped thinking about Thomas. I forgot about him like I forgot about the countless other men, young and old, who came and left for more reasons than I could ever remember. Months later, we found out Thomas was dead. He overdosed, and he died. I could not help thinking that Thomas had finally been released. He had been released from himself.

What had we done but abuse the most sacred of freedoms? We had abused our freedom of choice by choosing to poison ourselves at the expense of everyone and anyone. We were the embodiment of those who refuse all reason, and we were quite rightfully corralled into a space of confinement, and since this space of confinement could not come with the literal high walls that hid us from the world, we were given the digital stigmata to make us visible to those systems that would protect the world from us. We are not paraded before the public for entertainment, but we are more visible in the twenty-first century than any time in history. That set of sacred texts generated by the legal system, the medical system, educational institutions, psychiatric systems—all of this reveals us and writes us into a network of digital walls that render us visible in as many forms possible. We are the monsters of unreason made transparent by forms of knowledge that capture us, name us, describe and define us, and ultimately place us behind walls that can move around ahead of us wherever we may go.

Even as I move around in the world, the walls remain fixed ahead of and around me. Those accidental meetings with those I once knew, but who know a version of me, means to look at them through the walls, and I am aware that many of these people can see the walls better than I. They know. They know that I was there, with them, living among them, and then I was no longer. They know that I went to a place to be treated, to be rehabilitated, to find my way from the mute space of unreason and back to the realm of language and meaning. But we both know that I am one who has been to the space of unreason, and I carry the mark of insane, the debauched, the heretical, and the disorderly… "if they see me I am a monster of the solitudes he sees man for the first time and does not flee before him explorers bring home his skin among their trophies" (*How it is*, 13).

Becoming is a matter of insinuating myself at the margins of the multiple language games that render me visible as all that I am not through the language of unreason, the language of all that I am not but in which I find myself. That murmur beneath language and forms of language found anywhere I happen to find them. I do not justify or explain, take and bring in order to situate myself at the level of the passive in which I am not inactive, but I do acquiesce to anything at all. I retain my unreason while I present something that makes contact with the language games that are deemed appropriate. All the while, nothing will ever allow me to forget that I am one of the insane, the debauched, the heretical, and the disorderly. I am the monster of the solitudes.

The process of making amends in the Twelve Steps is in Steps 8 and 9. The process is quite involved:

> 8. Made a list of all persons we had harmed, and became willing to make amends to them all.
> 9. Made direct amends to such people wherever possible, except when to do so would injure them or others.

We are to work with an AA sponsor, someone who has worked the steps, and write down all the people we have harmed. We are to work out specific strategies for contacting these people and offer to make amends. A crucial feature of amends is that they are not apologies. We are not to approach people we harmed to apologize for our actions. We are to offer to do something tangible that the injured person will define, and we are to perform that tangible action to the best of our abilities. These steps are both selfless and, to some degree selfish. They are selfless because the specific nature of the amends is not determined by us, and we are going to the injured party with the details of the wrongs we did them. They are selfish because what we get out of it is a form of exoneration. We are not absolved of guilt, but we are absolved of the responsibility for our guilt. Even if the injured party wants nothing to do with us and refuses our attempts to make amends, once we have done these steps, we owe nothing to the injured party and we are exonerated. We are free to move about the world without the fear that our wrongs are still out there for us to confront.

Yet, I have never felt that things end either with the list of wrongs, the amends themselves, and the idea that we have attained a transformation of the state of things. People do not forget, and I strongly suspect that few people forgive. No matter the promises of the 12-step program, there are a few resentments I will never lose, and there are a few things I will never forgive. I expect nothing less from others.

Being out among "normal" people, especially those I had known in one way or another before the end, was to experience a sense of profound foreignness. As one who dwelt among the world of unreason, I really had no interest in finding a way to communicate with anyone. It was not a feeling of shame or being self-conscious, I simply did not want to be seen. I found that the people I encountered after the end were the ones who appeared uncomfortable, as if they did not really know how to talk to me anymore since I had clearly been marked off from them. The boundary that separated the House from the rest of the world existed on another plane. It was something that separated me from others by an insurmountable gulf, and I did not have any interest in reaching across this gulf. I was content to be forgotten, and I resented the fact that too often I was not forgotten.

From my journal, December 28, 2013:

> Where did everyone go? Was I really that bad? Am I invisible? Do I just appear in other peoples' dreams? When they wake up, do I fade into an unconscious, barred from the day to day? I spent my life dreaming and one day woke up in the same orphanage I started in. We come into the world alone, and we leave the world alone. I obviously left the world. Is this what it feels like to be dead?
> Where did everyone go?
> I had a terrible dream
> and when I awoke, I was all alone
> I dreamed the world was real and
> full of people who only knew me
> when I stood right in front of them.
> When I walked away
> I was all alone
> and then everyone went away

Aside from the poor attempt at verse, I can see the movement of my thoughts as I go from that period of shock and recognition of the blank of life to the passiveness of one who no longer wishes to be seen at all. Looking back at the "little private book these secret things little book all my own the heart's outpourings day by day it's forbidden one big book" (*How it is*, 84). And what will come but the willingness (if not the capability) to dwell in the passive, in that state which withdraws from the need or even desire of the reciprocal relations that render one a subject and an object; wishing only to be an objectless subject that is no longer recognized or named at all; allowing, or acquiescing, to the systems of naming and taxonomy that had already named me so as to remove myself entirely from those systems. Rather than being an addition to the world, I would be the result of a subtraction from the writing of myself that is now more real than myself. Leaving what remains of myself as the contents of a tomb. The writing of a self, as Blanchot says, is something of a death. What remains is the life that was even as the life that is continues. But what continues cannot be quite what preceded. There has been an exchange, and in the process of this exchange, something is lost, and something is made new. That which is new retains kernels of what was. That which is lost lives on only in the memento mori of what is entombed in the new. The writing that became what I appeared to be serves as a crypt which entombs what is left after the end. The crypt of writing—cryptogram. And thus, re-encrypting, or encrypting anew in the remains of other language fragments.

The café is busy. The downtown business people crowded in. People meeting others. Laptops out and notebooks laid out carefully along the side. Cell phones, pens, earbuds, coffee cups and small plates with the remnants of food… People deeply engrossed in what they are doing; others talking loudly; a man sits slumped back on one of the couches working a crossword puzzle. The homeless men out front with their cardboard signs and their paper cups. I stand in line and look around. I look mostly at the floor and wait for the line to move. And we see each other. Theirs is a furtive glance as if they did not want to make eye contact. I did not want to make eye contact. "How you been, man?" "Doing alright, and you?" Obligatory filler for a chance meeting no one wanted. Some small talk. Then they order, look at me quickly, nervously, "see you…" And that is it. We stand in distant places in the café to wait for our drinks. They make their way out quickly. We both know. Once out the door, I will fade from mind. As if I only exist when I am before their eyes. Once I disappear from sight, I no longer exist. Just like I have not existed for a long time. Just a ghost. All that once made us something other than what we are now—all that is nothing but ghosts.

> you are there somewhere alive somewhere vast stretch of time then it's over you are there no more alive no more then again you are there again alive again it wasn't over an error you begin again all over more or less in the same place or in another as when another image above in the light come to in hospital in the dark. (*How it is*, 22)

> Extimacy is not the contrary of intimacy. Extimacy says that the intimate is Other—like a foreign body, a parasite. (Jacques-Alain Miller, *The Symptom* 9, Fall 2008)

The time within the House progresses in its fashion. That monotonous day to day gives way to months, and the shock of the end gives way to something like routine and what one can call daily life. Within, and in large part under, this daily life, I emerged as… something… While life in the House did become ordinary to me, it never became something that gave me a feeling of living. "Life" in the House was always an in-between; it was always a space holder between what was and what may eventually come—some distant dream of something other than what is. Certainly, I had dreams of what my life could become. These ranged from schemes that were over-wrought with delusions of grandeur to bleak endings of a more final sort: jail or death. I filled my time with reading and writing. I developed programs of reading I never pursued with any diligence, and I began projects that I never completed, some ended almost as quickly as they started. What did emerge, simply by the logic of chance and necessity, were encounters with an exterior wherein I seemed to discover what would stand for a self. This was not a process of identification. I did not read these things and directly identify with characters, ideas, stories, or details. I encountered a version of myself in fragments and pieces of things I read.

At first, I attempted to directly channel these texts into writing projects. This failed at every turn, although the attempts had value I could not then see. The exterior I encountered in writing founded an interior I did not know was shaping into a ghost within me that I would one day encounter as myself.

From my journal, August 3, 2014:

> I started writing. "The Divine Miranda," from *Godot*. Miranda means "wonder." Shakespeare coined the name. On the eve of 11 months, in my cozy monk's cell, resolved to many things, a beautiful night, I suddenly feel compelled to write, and finding all the necessary pieces, I begin the Miranda. In the absence of an other in my life, in my solitary state in the world, I can begin to create an other. The Chief of Birds can send his words to the only object-image that can make him feel love. Nothing more than a defect in the perfection of non-being, he finds his love in the words that invent love. Afflicted with the stigmata and with loneliness. He is Prospero trapped in Caliban. And he is no hero of the pastoral. Just a demon slipping and sneaking from word to word.

Most significant to these ramblings is the near random association of references which had ceased to be distinguished based on their origins. The need to make reference to something from within its textual space of origin had faded, and I had begun the process of regenerating these scraps and fragments as features of an exterior that would be taken in as an interior. As the world that is the House took place around me, and the world beyond the House became increasingly alien to me, the interior spaces of other interior spaces became the world that was becoming.

Yet, even as I consciously and deliberately decided to aim in a direction of almost pure textuality, I was not entirely capable of entombing the flesh that is my body and all that this entails. What appeared to come about was, and remains, a split. I suspect, but cannot really know, that this split has always been the case. I can only suspect because I write from within. I cannot know if this has always been the case because what was is foreclosed to me, is entombed like all other memories that precede the end since all these memories are now accessed through the opaque disaster that was the end. "The crack: a fissure which could be constitutive of the self, or would reconstitute itself as the self, but not as a cracked self" (*The Writing of the Disaster*, 78).

The House takes on its own sense of "normal." The general hum of daily life, the longer I stayed, became the same indistinguishable background that is any life. But I never reached a point at which I considered life in the House normal. I never lost sight of the fact that I lived in an institution, and that the problem of becoming institutionalized loomed over me and everyone else as an ever-present feature of what could become.

The House is exceptional for a number of reasons, and one of these reasons is the fact that people can and do stay at the House for extremely long periods. There are people who will never leave the House. They can no longer function in the world beyond. There are many reasons for this. There are some men who come to the House after a lifetime of struggles that cannot be properly described. There are men who were simply throw-away humans almost from birth and lived their lives on the streets doing whatever it took to survive. They spent their lives stealing, hustling, selling their own bodies, and their lives were characterized by forms of violence few of us can imagine. For these men, drugs and alcohol were as much a part of life as food and shelter. There were no lessons from well-meaning schoolteachers on the dangers of drugs and alcohol. There were no parents to come home to and face the music after a night of drinking with friends. There was nothing for them but bare meager survival. Since nearly all these men had extensive criminal records, most of which stretched back to early childhood, the fact that they made it to the House at all was nothing short of a miracle. And they will never find a place in the world outside, because there is no place for them in the world outside. There never was a place for them. To spend the rest of their lives sleeping indoors, eating hot food, and having access to a television was all they could ever want or need. To simply be left in relative peace—this is all they wanted. Some of these men held jobs outside the House, but most of them lived on some kind of public assistance. They filled small roles in the House as deskmen or in the kitchen. A small number of them remained hidden even within the House.

For others, the House was a temporary burden to fulfill the demands of the court. They were there to do their mandatory year of drug and alcohol treatment, they left as soon as they could. Few of these men stayed sober, and many of them died. A high percentage of them never made it through their year and were taken out of the House in handcuffs to do their prison time. There were many men who fit into this group.

And the rest of us were common drunks and drug addicts. It seemed the heroin addicts outnumbered the common drunks like me. Heroin is everywhere now; it is not some kind of urban problem. A good many of the heroin addicts were affluent young men from suburban homes who had tumbled out of their privileged little worlds into the life of being a junkie, complete with everything that often comes with being a junkie. Living on the streets, stealing, tricking— you name it. Good American boys who had seen a side of life they never knew could exist. For those of us who were of the common alcoholic variety, we came in a number of stripes. The men who had fucked up their successful lives and families and just needed to get things back on a good path were few. They never impressed me as likely to remain sober. They were more afraid of ending up like me. They were doing something drastic to simply make sure they would never end up like me, but many of them would in time. Then there were those like me. We had destroyed everything. The hopelessness I would see in these men's faces became so common it became boring. I could never bring myself to tell them things would somehow be alright, because I did not believe that even for myself. We were at the end, and for those who chose to simply go back out and see if they could get it over with, I never blamed them. I saw too many guys pick back up anyway because there was just no way out for them. They were never going to be sober.

All of this made up the common din of everyday life. All of us wandering from one thing to the next with nothing to expect but more of the same. Each day had its structure. We knew what we were going to do on Tuesday because we did the same thing every Tuesday, and the only things that made Tuesday different from any other day were the specific types of the same things we did on those days. It becomes so common you never need to think anymore, and above all else, you were discouraged from ever thinking. This is the nature of all institutional life. It is about routine and habit. Eventually, the routine and habit of the institution becomes a part of yourself. At this point, you are not a separate individual—a self, you are a part of the institution, a piece of the construction that makes the institution what it is. I lived in terror of this happening to me. I knew that if I became institutionalized, I would completely cease to exist forever.

I remained in the House for as long as I did because there was nothing else for me. I had no money, and I had no real prospect for making money, at least not enough money to live outside the House. I had no family. And the prospect of taking up residence with someone outside the House was reprehensible to me, as it was to anyone I may have known prior to coming to the end. I stayed, and I lived in the House as if it was my home. A constant fear for me, the more I grew accustomed to life in the House, was the problem of becoming institutionalized. The process whereby one comes to completely understand themselves only within the context of institutional life. That I would reach a point at which I could no longer see myself, my being, my sense of self as separable from the life that is the House. Experience, life, and the constitution of a self can cut in at least two ways: "The crack: a fissure which could be constitutive of the self, or would reconstitute itself as the self, but not as a cracked self" can manifest itself as a fundamental misrecognition of the patterns, culture, daily habits, and common modes of understanding that determine the House. All of this can become constitutive of my self in such a way that I lose touch with whatever form of a self I believed to be constituting on my own (Blanchot, *The Writing of the Disaster*, 78). At which point, I am not a self, but an extension of institutional practices and the culture specific to an institution. We see this in people who have spent decades in prison. After so much time, they no longer recognize the world outside and can no longer find themselves in the world outside. No longer behind bars, they are nonetheless imprisoned in the institutional culture of being a prisoner. What is the critical point at which this occurs? As with language acquisition and the window of opportunity for the acquisition of language, at what point are we inaugurated into a mode of being that is that of the institution and forever locked out of what lies beyond the institution? "Yes, my past has thrown me out, its gates have slammed behind me, or I burrowed my way out alone, to linger a moment free in a dream of days and nights, dreaming of me moving, season after season, towards the last, like the living, till suddenly I was here, all memory gone" (Beckett, *Texts for Nothing*, 8). Once that door or window slams behind me, I am here forever even in my dreams, even in the idea of beyond here that I concoct in journals, in daydreams, in the brief contact I make with what is beyond. The world that is the House becomes what I am, and the self that is constituted by me is not constituted by me at all. What is left is "nothing but fantasies and hope of a story for me somehow, of having come from somewhere of being able to go back, or on, somehow, some day, or without hope" (*Texts for Nothing*, 8).

Another possibility is to refuse the House in my everyday life. To find within myself, more precisely, to find the language of how to be from an outside that cannot be touched by anyone but me. To build a world, to constitute a self from the places and spaces and fragments where I find myself anyway, "but not as a cracked self." Do not make sense to this place. Never be one who can be accessed by the language that defines the culture of the House. Even the broken pieces of what remained of me needed to be further fractured—fractalized—into something that will remain illegible to the world within which I existed but which I desperately needed to remain fissured but not cracked. The systems of language and the writing of me that existed in excess of me would never denote the tomb that encased me. It would only ever denote the cenotaph while me "I" would always be elsewhere.

In the course of both Stage I and II of treatment, there is never a point at which one can disengage and simply live life as an independent person. We are endlessly told that AA is a "we program," and the idea of retreating into yourself is considered the first order of selfishness and self-centeredness. We must always remain actively engaged. There are always new men coming into the House, and they need the help and guidance of group members who are further along in their recovery. We guide them through step work, help them adjust to the demands of the House, we are still given daily chores like cleaning details. This last gives rise to an internal economy of the House. Some guys will pay other guys to do their chores. Some will even pay you to do their laundry. At one point, I made about 50 bucks a week doing other guys' chores and laundry. In any case, we must at all times be actively involved in the daily life of the House no matter what we may think of ourselves and our own lives. Yet, as time went on, I became increasingly withdrawn into a world, life, and selfhood of my own creation that was an antithesis of the demands of the House. But I nevertheless remained an active participant in the House. I saw it as the process of metonymy. Whatever I presented of myself to others was always a small part of the whole that I managed to present as the whole. This is what it means to become the neutral, the passive rather than the active speaking subject presumed to be prior to the end and the disaster, and this is what will remain even to this day. What emerged from the beginning of the end, and still remains, is "utter uprootedness, exile, the impossibility of presence, dispersion (separation)" (*The Writing of the Disaster*, 18).

Remaining in the House means the flows and lines that define the world that is the House necessarily interrupt, decode, and re-code the self. I become the House as the House becomes whatever it is that is my self, which is to say I lose my self in the House. I become unmoored from the flows and lines of consistency that I believed made me. Losing myself in the House even if I do resist the process of institutionalization; I am the institution to the extent that a micro-world is made of those monads that absorb, redirect, and define from within that world.

From my journal, March 16, 2014:

> "in a universe suddenly divested of illusion and lights, man feels an alien, a stranger. His exile is without remedy since he is deprived of the memory of a lost home or the hope of a promised land." Camus.
>
> Memory and hope are both illusions that function as realities only when these are threaded to objects which give materiality to the greater narrative which these illusions support. The system is dialectical and reciprocal. Memories are experienced as real because they are constantly re-infused with meaning by the narrative. The narrative can only continue to unfold if it is tied to hope. Take any significant feature out of the dialectic and the whole thing implodes. In this condition of radical alienation, I can only experience loss itself. I become a stranger in itself. Not a stranger

"from" or "to," but a stranger only. All of my memories are markers of loss and therefore unreal and gone. There is no hope of a promised land. No promise of anything at all. In this state, I cut through the Absurd man and become an abyss—a ghost. Others can still see and hear me, but as soon as I am no longer registered by their senses, I am no longer there, here, or present in any way.

Exile means to be without a home and without a destination. In this place where I am, my home is not even a memory, it is a distant idea that has no real reference. And the home that serves as a home is not a home except insofar as it is a "home" in the institutional sense of the term: a home for the homeless, an orphans' home, an old-folks' home… I cannot conceive of a destination at least in part because I do not want one. I am an exile, a nomad who is not, in between everything and simply exists in motion. My exile is internal. Even in the House, I am a function of a metonymic process by which the fragments that are pieced together to form my "I" are only accessible in atomized forms since the whole is a priori rejected as unacceptable. I speak and communicate to others in the form of symbols that hide the condensed content. My relation to others is the dream work. Even what I once took to be an internal and essential substance is now a disjointed set of relations with words and language games that are not my own and certainly not my self. I am without place or destination within the sense of self. That fundamental relation in which same and other correspond so as to give meaning to the subject/object relation is unstable and indeterminate.

In the meeting room that doubles as a tv room. Education. We sit and listen to a man whose only qualification is that he is a sober alcoholic who passed through the House years ago.

He speaks to us as one who knows—just knows. He knows all there is to know, and he makes it clear to us that our lives depend on listening to his words. He tells us the Big Book was written by God. He asks us to cite passages from the Big Book, and we do cite them exactly, and he tells us we are wrong. We sit and stare at him blankly as he adopts a voice designed to resemble a down-home preacher. On it goes, and we know that to grumble or argue or in any way object is to exert self-will and ego, and these are signs that we will certainly die an alcoholic death. And barring this inevitable and tragic death, we will be written up and put on restriction for our failure to show respect for a man who is selflessly devoting himself to our edification and continued sobriety. I stare out one of the three windows. I can see one old tree, leafless in late autumn; I see the picnic table. In the distance I can see the back porch of one of the ¾ houses. Sometimes I see one of the ¾ guys walk past the window, and I envy his freedom. I listen and I don't listen. It takes nothing to hear the inane words and dismiss them as soon as I hear them. And while I hear the words, I am somewhere else within. I am in this room, and the world within which I must exist has its own internal paradigm of thought, even if this paradigm is modeled after the dominant modes of thought that define the world beyond this place. It is possible, and quite simple really, to appropriate the schema of how thought functions and then backfill the content with language that coheres only according to an accepted set of meanings within the closed system. This will resemble logic and reason, but it has no coherence beyond the internal system. To operate according to this system, you need only learn the language and key terms and speak them in ways that adhere to the schema of logic but contain the meanings created from within the internal system. In this way, I could speak the language of the internal modes of meaning and understanding in the House while fighting to maintain a sense of meaning, logic, and reason that exceeds the House. But I, or anyone, must never confuse the two systems or ever, under any circumstances, attempt to evaluate the internal system and paradigm against external modes of meaning. This is self-will and will lead to relapse and death. Another option is to accept the meaningless internal system and the fact that the external system does not include me since my being has been extracted and abstracted into other systems of meaning and understanding, other paradigms. In these systems, I am only the writing of the system. In this case, another mode of meaning arises. Or, it is more accurate to say that what I found were fragments of other systems of meaning, and I assembled them in ways that had meaning only for me. And I still do. Take language and language systems, accept systems of meaning only as provisional and contingent systems, and never accept the idea that there is something beyond these systems that hold them together. In which case, words, language, writing, systems of meaning—all exist purely to be used as a mobile set of signs and symbols that can be appropriated and assembled in any way imaginable without ever reaching for justification.

I long for the day when I too will be free and living in the ¾ house. A cloud of pieces of memories float through my mind as I drift away from the speaker and his inane drone. After 13 months in the House, I walk by the same window. I can hear the same speaker addressing a group of new guys and saying the same utterly inane (and even insane) things. And I long for a time when I will be free. I am completely free. Free from... I am never free. The picnic table remains empty. The tree remains. Leafless in late autumn.

Exile is not simply the condition of being removed from a homeland. Exile is internal; it is the condition of being dislocated from the internal points of rootedness. The habits and routines of existence within the heterotopic space will inevitably take hold in the deepest parts of the mind and imagination. Just as the dead in the cemetery remain present only to the extent that their absence is permanently marked with signs of absence, so those whose lives are defined within the heterotopia become absent beings whose lives are marked by the languages of absence. Most of the guys in the House who managed to claw their way back to the outside worked just as hard at re-establishing themselves as present in the world. Many of them had good reasons—reasons that were never really gone for them. Family ties, homes, the narrative of a once uninterrupted existence—all of this was still intact for them, and they spent their time in the House struggling to re-enter this flow of "normality." For others, the moment of the end when we crossed the threshold represented by the House marked the final cut. For me, it revealed the fact that what was experienced as loss was in fact the awareness of lack. Home, or anything that could stand for a home, had been such a distant abstraction for so long, I no longer missed anything, and I found that I was not seeking anything like home.

The long walks and urban hikes had become such a source of liberation that they eventually became the only place I felt like I belonged. To lack a destination was the goal, and this tendency remains part of me to this day. The nomad is not one who wanders from one place to another. The nomad is one who is caught in the unmapped space of being in between and finds the peace of rootedness in the non-contingent space of movement. It is more than moving away from being in a place. It was moving away from having a place—from being present.

> I have to speak, whatever that means. Having nothing to say, no words but the words of others, I have to speak. (*The Unnamable*, 314)

Beyond the two Stages of treatment in the House, I could choose to remain within the life of the House in what is called ¾ housing. This is housing on the premises in which we are no longer under the strict control of the House but remain as residents of the House. We pay rent to the House and we remain members of the community within the House. We can still take meals in the Hall. We still enjoy the safety the House affords us as recovering people. And we are expected to remain involved in the community of recovery that is the House. We go to meetings, both in-house and around the city. We have complete freedom to come and go. We can even have visitors. In some cases, men have others live with them in their rooms. I knew one man whose son came to live with him in ¾ housing. I knew several men who invited their wives and girlfriends to take up residence in these single rooms. It is a great relief to make it to ¾ housing. Most guys leave the House once their year is up. The men who are there to serve out the conditions of the court get out as fast as they can. Many of them go right back the lives they led before coming to the House, complete with their drug of choice. Others are simply sick of living under the weight of the House. After thirteen months, I took my place in ¾ housing.

I was in my first ¾ housing room for only about three months. It was a tiny space, barely enough room for a single bed and a dresser to fit side by the side. It had a closet with no door on one end. The wall was rotted through to the outside, and when we got heavy rain, water would pour through the wall as if someone was holding a hose up to it, soaking one side of the room, and I did not care. I was happy to be out from under the weight of the constant surveillance and monitoring, the constant need of counselors and others to find problems and make me pay for them, the danger at every moment that I would be put on restriction and forced to stay in the House during all my free time. I felt free.

After about three months I moved into a nicer room in a different house. It was larger, drier, and felt like a perfect little monk's cell to hide in for months or years or the rest of my life. I could not say at the time. There are two windows on one wall that face out to the house next door. Another window on the wall adjacent faces out to the yard behind the house. I have a small single bed against the wall opposite the two windows. A closet to the right of the bed. My furniture, in addition to the bed, consists of a dresser, a long folding table, and a rather larger wooden table that I use primarily as a writing desk, but I also eat on this table. Above the desk/table, there is a set of metal cabinets that were once kitchen cabinets from when my room had once been a kitchen. The outline of a sink remains on the wall with chipped and peeling paint. In the center of the cabinets there is a small shelf that I decorated with old postcards found in random places, playing cards, odds and ends found on walks, and about six Hispanic devotional candles I bought at a grocery store. I rarely light them. The desk is lined across the wall with books. It is strewn with papers—scraps of notes, beginnings of things I will never finish, junk mail and serious mail that I ignore. I have an electric guitar and a small practice amplifier that I keep near the desk. I also have an old metal fan.

I do all I can to transform my room in ¾ housing into a monk's cell. I keep it dark at all times using only lamps, never overhead light. I detest overhead light to this day. At night, I keep two small lamps on. The room is bathed in darkness and soft light. I listen to the classical music radio station whenever

I am home on an old radio I found in the basement of the House. And I read, and I write. Most of my writing is in journals, but I acquired a computer by the time I got to ¾ housing, and I write stories, poems, longer experiments that are complete failures and are long lost. Most of what I wrote during this time, with the exception of the journals, is lost. I spend nearly all my free time either alone in my room, alone in cafés, or going on long walks around the city. And while I come to enjoy my solitude, I never really attained the attitude of a solitary monk. There are parts of me that cling and will not die off. I feel the need to speak, and I am unable to keep silence.

With this small step toward living, if not quite in the world, at least a step toward having access to the world, I inevitably open the space for the world to have access to me. I am exposed for the first time since the end. I found that I resisted this exposure in ways that felt almost primitive. While my first days and weeks in the House were filled with fragmentary and incoherent fantasies of "normal" life, I now found that I had no interest in anything that may fit into the category of normal, that I had been removed from the world in such a profound way that life beyond the end was a source of fear even as I felt a kind of reverse pride that suggests that the world no longer deserved to have access to me. I say life beyond the end because I definitely desired life beyond the House. As much as ¾ housing offered freedoms and autonomy I had not known for many years, between the descent into madness and the time of the end, I did feel a powerful need to move beyond this final Stage of life in the House. But I no longer wanted anything to do with things as they are or were, and I had come to see myself as distinct from all those people I had once known. Amends, for example, remained a priority in the most perfunctory forms. I really did not care what people thought of me, and I genuinely believed they had no way to accurately think anything of me.

I did begin to wonder if I had become institutionalized, if I had so internalized the heterotopic and institutional life that had engulfed me that I no longer understood how to function in the world I had once considered to be so ordinary. But I also came to a place at which I did not care. I was not a part of the House, because I had resisted it so deeply, and I was no longer a part of the common world because I had been irrevocably separated from it. I wanted to remain silent, to remain in the spaces that emerged between what I read, wrote, and spun from dreams while walking. I spent long spans of any given evening listening to music and staring blankly. Picking up bits of things to read without focusing on them. Writing things and deleting them. Of course, I had access to social media, but this only furthered the sense of alienation. But maybe alienation is not the correct word. I did not feel alienated. I felt detached not just from people and ways of life, but from the very ideas of people and ways of life, and the only problem I sensed was that I could never be solitary enough.

In the world outside, I always felt like I was performing myself, like I was never really *being* myself so much as I was enacting *a self*. Perhaps this is just life, and the profound separation I experienced with coming to the end made this fact so starkly evident that I could no longer slip into that apparently natural way of being and remained always aware of the script and the audience. In any case, I had no interest in keeping up the performance and longed only to find a place and condition of pure solitude. And while I was, on some level, happy to be among people, I also had no desire to have them in my life. Everyone I had known before the end had become more other than other. They were an other that did not correspond to my same.

From my journal, February 3, 2015:

> Do not talk. Do not think. Do not analyze. Withdraw! Do not Be. A light shines on everything, not just the specific object. In much the same way, any central point is always at the periphery of another circle. The "I" is only real to the extent that one accepts the internal centrality of the self, when in fact, this perception of centrality is ephemeral in the cloud of being full of other "I's." It is all a matter of narrative games. And every move in each game is always lost.
>
> I felt myself getting away from myself, and I pulled back into myself with intensity. So much intensity that one small feature of me became all of me. Why is it that rage becomes so familiar and easy? It is a comfortable pair of baggy jeans that I can belt around me no matter how big or small I may actually be.
>
> I know it's not the style, but I just don't care. But care is a thing I do and a thing I have. Can I give up both? Do I stop the progress of verb, and in doing, dislodge the noun? The noun is a general category. There are specific examples, but this involves the problem of degree. The verb is variably invested depending on specific care. It comes down to a system of value, and therefore an economy. Do I give up certain particulars so as to lighten the load of others, and thus reduce the momentum of the verb? The rhetorical questions serve as rehearsals for an anticipated action—another verb to supplant or supersede the verb in question. Thus, the economy of care plays out as a drama—a performance, and therefore a fiction. Which rhetorical drama of an alternative verb is variously convincing?

> Alternatives can be tested. Do I tend toward the sociopath or the Quixotic psychotic?

It is hard to make any real sense of all this. What remains clear, and what pertains to the space I tried and needed to create, was the commitment to rendering myself to myself within the cloud of language with which I had immersed myself. I was neither here nor anywhere else, and I did not find myself in either. I found myself in the words of others. "Having nothing to say, no words but the words of others, I have to speak" (*The Unnamable*, 314). I have to speak, but I cannot speak anything other than what others have spoken (written) before me. Having lost myself, I began to emerge as otherness. After more than a year of treatment, of life in the House, of having myself undone by an endless net of language systems, I gained traction by latching onto the fragmentary languages of others, and not just any others, but the fragmentary language of the fragmentary. The ways of presenting myself to others, because this was inevitable, was to cloak myself in the things I latched onto to create a language for myself without ever revealing the absence that remained within. I learned to speak but not to communicate myself, to cloak the silence I could not keep.

Nothing ever comes from the outside, and there is an inside and an outside. The time spent living in a space outside of places made it clear to me that there is a space in which the world dwells, and there is a space within that space in which I and the others in the House exist. Most important, I learned that there is no path, no connecting access point from one to the other. Once I crossed the end, I crossed an invisible line that only exists in the moment of its passing. It is a step beyond, into the beyond. In AA, this is referred to as "the spiritual experience." The Big Book, in one of the appendices, explains that for most of us, "our experiences are what the psychologist William James calls the 'educational variety' because they develop slowly over a period of time." People within the 12-step community like to extol the beauty of the spiritual experience. The step into the end constituted a break with what was—what is. And the years that followed, not that they unfolded as time in any conventional sense, provided something of an educational variety of experience, an experience that allowed a separation that already existed to become apparent.

Blanchot writes "that the end is always premature, that it is the haste of the Finite to which one longs to entrust oneself once and for all without foreseeing that the Finite is only the ebb of the Infinite" (*The Writing of the Disaster*, 31). The end was just an opening, a space or absence. The end was, and still is, that empty present which is always receding into absence. The step into this absent space, though never made present by myself to myself, was nevertheless made known by the words of others. My path away and out was to allow myself to be stitched together from broken pieces of the words of others. Even now, years later and far from the House, I am never fully present.

Michael Templeton is an independent scholar and writer. He completed his Ph.D. in literary studies at Miami University of Ohio in 2005. He has written creative non-fiction and critical essays on contemporary culture, which have been published in online and print magazines and journals. He lives in West Milton, Ohio with his wife who is an artist.

PREVIOUSLY PUBLISHED AT ERRATUM PRESS

Lord of Chaos
Daniel Beauregard

If I Had Not Seen Their Sleeping Faces
Christina Tudor-Sideri

The Prodigious Earth
Eric Blix

Morant
Roy Goddard

bone bite snare
Michael Mc Aloran

Last Days of Pompeii. Vol.1
Steve Hanson

PUBLISHED BY ERRATUM REPRINTS

The Scourge of Villanie
John Marston
Civilisation Its Cause and Cure
Edward Carpenter

www.ingramcontent.com/pod-product-compliance
Lightning Source LLC
Chambersburg PA
CBHW030305100526
44590CB00012B/530